SOCCER COACHING
MADE EASY...

A Coach's Guide to
Youth Player Development

by Tom Goodman, M. Ed.
President - World Class Soccer

**Library of Congress
Cataloging in Publication Data**

by Thomas Goodman, M. Ed.
   Soccer Coaching Made Easy
   A Coach's Guide to Youth Player Development
ISBN No. 1 59164 101 2
Library of Congress Control Number: 2005931311

Cover Design
Bryan R. Beaver

Diagrams made with
easySportsGraphics
www.sports graphics.com

Cover Photo by
© J. Knorr Photography

Printed by
DATA REPRODUCTIONS
Auburn, Michigan

Reedswain Publishing
562 Ridge Road
Spring City, PA 19475
800.331.5191
www.reedswain.com
info@reedswain.com

Table of Contents

<u>Acknowledgements</u>

I would like to thank the many State Directors of Coaching in the USA that have both directly and indirectly contributed to this book. Our many discussions at soccer coaching meetings and events about youth player development inspired me to pursue this project.

I would like to thank all of the people who coached me through the years, especially my high school coach, Lee Kenworthy, who put special meaning into the phrase "player development". His organization and attention to detail has stayed with me throughout my soccer career.

I would like to thank Ed Tremble, a friend and mentor, who pulled me back into the game at a very crucial time in my life. His love of the game and his outstanding ability to teach young players continues to be incomparable.

I would like to thank my parents, Jimmy and Dora Goodman, for letting me experience the game of soccer on my own and for always supporting my efforts as a player and a coach.

Finally, I want to thank my lovely wife, Michelle, for her help and tremendous understanding as I pursued a career in Youth Soccer. Her patience and strength were paramount to my humble successes in the game.

Welcome to Youth Coaching

The position of *youth soccer coach* is a very important one. You are charged with the responsibility of positively impacting the development of young people using the sport of soccer...an awesome responsibility.

The youth soccer coach must work toward providing each player in his charge with an environment conducive to learning and having FUN! This is no small task. It will take effective management of players, parents, referees and opponents to provide such an environment. Preparation for training sessions and games is imperative if positive player development is the goal.

The decisions that you make as a youth coach may not always be popular decisions, but if they are player-development-centered, they will be the RIGHT decisions. With that in mind, I have prepared this Youth Player Development Manual to assist you in your efforts to be the best coach that you can be.

Good luck!

Tom Goodman, M.Ed.
President

World Class Soccer

How to Use This Manual

The manual that you are about to use is organized into the following major *Sections* as detailed in the Table of Contents:

The **Age Group** sections are full of valuable information such as:

✓ Role of the coach
✓ Age group player characteristics
✓ What game components should be taught to players in the age group
✓ What the training session should look like for players in the age group
✓ Sample training sessions for the age group
✓ Appropriate activities for the age group
✓ Coaching considerations (what can be coached) for each activity

The **Coaching Considerations** section is separated into two sub-sections:

Technique
Coaching points for teaching the mechanics of dribbling, receiving, kicking (passing & shooting), heading and tackling.

Tactics
Coaching considerations when teaching the **"decision making"** part of the game.

The way to use this manual:

- ✓ Locate the age group section that you are interested in.
- ✓ Read the section carefully.
- ✓ Determine what activities you would like to use for your next training session.
- ✓ Determine the coaching considerations that you would like to teach from the list included with each activity.
- ✓ Refer to the *Coaching Considerations Section* for detailed information on technical and tactical coaching points.

There are over 100 training activities illustrated in this book. The activities are universal in nature which means that most of them can be used at any age. The U10 and U12 age group activities can easily be used at older age groups…it all has to do with what you expect from your players.

Managing Your Team

Parent Meeting

Schedule a **parent meeting** before your first practice. The meeting can be in a formal setting or it can be part of a fun event, like a picnic or parent-player game.

Topics to be covered in the meeting include:

- ♦ *Your coaching philosophy*
  - Player development
    - Players exposed to different positions
    - Skill development
    - Positive environment
    - Foster creativity
    - Age appropriate activities
  - Enjoyment
    - Fun activities
    - Smiles and appropriate humor

- ♦ *Your expectations and goals for the season*

- ♦ *Player responsibilities*

  - ✓ Arriving at all training sessions and games prepared to work hard and have Fun!
  - ✓ Helping with field/equipment set up or break down when appropriate
  - ✓ Bringing water and shin pads to training sessions and games

- ♦ *Parents' responsibilities*

  - ▪ Getting players to practices and games promptly
  - ▪ Being supportive of their children and the team
  - ▪ Exhibiting positive behavior at training and games
  - ▪ Focusing on player development and fun rather than winning or losing
  - ▪ Communication assistance (phone/email chain when practices or games are changed)
  - ▪ Helping to get medical assistance if necessary

- Providing refreshments
- Helping with field/equipment set up or break down

Equipment

Players	*Team*
Soccer ball	Cones, extra soccer balls, air pump
Shin guards	Colored pinnies (bibs, vests)
Soccer shoes	Safe playing surface
Appropriate clothing	First aid kit
Water bottle	Ice and plastic sandwich bags

Player Development

The U6 Age Group

The fascination for the ball, the desire to play with it and the thrill of scoring goals provides the entrance into a lifetime of soccer participation. The joy and pleasure of the game are best nurtured by encouraging freedom of expression and organizing play in small groups.

Role of the U6 Coach

The role of the coach in the U6 age group is that of facilitator, friendly helper, organizer, and motivator. The coach should be patient, enthusiastic, and imaginative. The coach should experiment with fun activities that include all players, if possible. The environment and the activities are more important than technical coaching at this level.

License Requirement

The U6/U8 State Youth Module is required. The National Youth License is recommended.

The U6 Player Characteristics

Mental/Psychological (cognitive)

Short attention span
Individually oriented...egocentric
Sensitive...Easily bruised psychologically
Love to use their imagination...pretend
Tend to only one task at a time
Can process small bits of information
Immature understanding of time and space relations

Physical (psychomotor)

Constantly in motion
No sense of pace (full speed ahead)
Easily fatigued with rapid recovery
Eye/hand and eye/foot coordination is primitive
Can balance on good foot
Catching skills are not developed
Love to run, jump, fall and roll
About 36-40 inches in tall
Weigh between 30-50 pounds

Socially (psychosocial)

Love to show off
Little or no real concern for team activities
Tend to parallel play...play next to but not with a friend or teammate
Influential person in their life is their MOM
Like to mimic goofy actions

Boys and girls are quite similar psychologically and physically.

What to Teach U6 Players
(Game Components)

Techniques (skills):

Dribbling
> Keep the ball close (with toe and inside of foot).
> Moves…stop & go and ½ turns.

Kicking
> Kicking the ball at the goal (with toe, inside of foot, and laces).

Catching
> Toss to self and catch.

Psychology (mental and social):
- Sharing
- Fair play
- Dealing with parental involvement (confusion)
- "How to play"
- Emotional management

Fitness (movement education):
- Balance
- Running
- Jumping
- Rolling
- Hopping
- Skipping

Tactics (decisions):
- Where is the field
- Moving in the correct direction (which goal to kick at)
- Dealing with the ball rolling away
- Dealing with the ball rolling toward

Rules:

The kick off
The goal kick
Ball in and out of play
Hand ball
Physical fouls (pushing, holding, striking, tripping)

US Youth Soccer Modifications to The Game

Playing numbers: 3 v 3 (no goalkeepers)
Field Dimensions:
    Length   20-30 yards
    Width   15-20 yards
Goal Dimensions:

    Height   6 feet
    Width   18 feet
Duration: four 8-minute quarters
Ball: number 3

Possible Formations

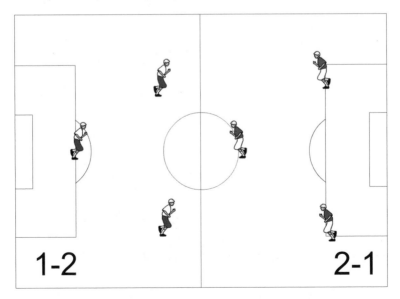

1-2   2-1

The Training Session

General Information

- ✓ The training session should involve fun and imaginative game like activities.
- ✓ Facilitate fun activities that draw out the skill in the player.
- ✓ Small-sided games such as 1 v 1, 2 v 1, 2 v 2, should be included as well.
- ✓ Training should always conclude with a 3 v 3 game without goalkeepers if possible.
- ✓ The duration of the training session should be 45-60 minutes.

Lesson Plan Design

The U6 training session should consist of 7-10 activities. There should be a mixture of dynamic, relaxation and dynamic competitive activities. The design would be as follows:

1. Dynamic Activity
2. Dynamic Activity
3. Relaxation Activity
4. Dynamic Activity
5. Relaxation Activity
6. Dynamic Competitive Activity
7. Dynamic Competitive Activity

Sample Lesson Plan

1. Fetch
2. In and Out
3. Try This
4. Gate Dribbling
5. Soccer Marbles
6. Sharks and Minnows
7. The Game 3 v 3

U6 Training Activities Table

Relaxation	Dynamic	Dynamic Competitive
Try This (I Can Do This…Can You?)	Line-to-Line Dribbling	Everybody's IT
Toe-Toe-Heel-Heel	Dribbling with Moves	Sharks and Minnows
Edge of the World	Interactive Dribbling	Cops and Robbers (Knock-Out)
Coordination Exercise 1-2-3-4	Fetch (Ball Toss)	Get Outta' There
Soccer Marbles (Hit the Balls)	Red Light-Green Light (Stop and Go)	Boss of the Balls (2 v 2)
Score a Goal (Meg the Coach)	Body Part Dribbling (Stop and Go)	The Game 3 v 3
Controlled Juggling	Musical Soccer Balls	
	Hit the Dirt (Low Flying Airplanes)	
	Gate Dribbling	
	Cross-Over Dribbling	
	In and Out	
	Relay Challenge	
	Kicking for Distance	
	Cone Kicking	
	Point Line	

U6 Training Activities

Relaxation Activities

♦ Try This (I Can Do This…Can You?)

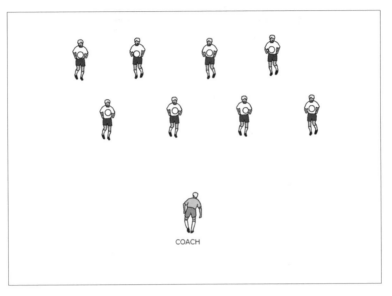

COACH

Equipment: One ball per player (if necessary).

Set-up: Open area; no boundaries.

Activity: The coach does something that will challenge the players without using a soccer ball. (i.e. balancing on one foot, leaning forward, arms spread as if flying and the other leg extended in back) The coach then says, "Try This!" or "I can do this…can you?". The players try to copy the coach. After trying a few things without the soccer ball, the coach can introduce the soccer ball and continue the activity in the same manner. (i.e. throwing the ball up in the air, clapping hands once or twice and catching the ball before it hits the ground)

Variations:
Without a soccer ball:
- Jump up and bring knees to chest, then land on feet.
- Star jumps…jump up with feet and arms outstretched, then land on feet.

11

With a soccer ball:

- ✓ Sit on the ground with legs outstretched and roll the ball on the ground around the feet, then around the back (circular pattern).
- ✓ Juggle the ball with one thigh, then catch it. Now try to juggle the ball from one thigh to the other, then catch it.

Coaching Considerations:

Fun, challenging, movement education, creativity, decision making.

◆ Toe-Toe-Heel-Heel

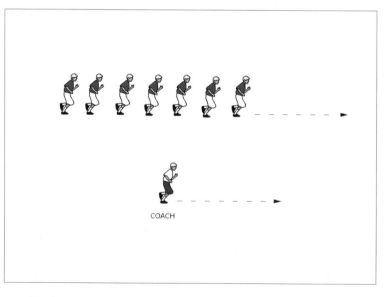

COACH

Equipment:	None
Set-up:	Open area; no boundaries. Players line up in single file. The coach is positioned to the side of the line
Activity:	The coach instructs the players to walk in a single file line. He then asks them to walk way up on their toes, then on their heels, then on the outsides of their feet, then on the insides of their feet, then like a duck, then like a pigeon and finally the coach asks them to flick their feet

After the players understand the various foot surfaces, the coach then introduces a chant as they walk:

"Toe-toe-heel-heel-outside-outside-inside-inside-duck-duck-pigeon-pigeon-flick-flick-flick-flick".

Repeat 3-4 times.

Coaching Considerations:

Movement education; balance; understanding the surfaces of the foot; FUN!

◆ Edge of the World

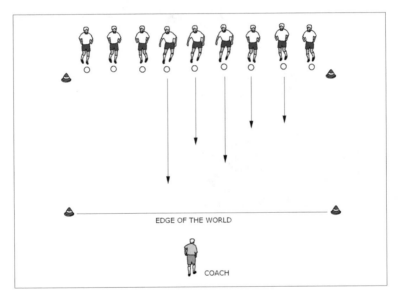

Equipment:	One ball per player. Cones.
Set-up:	Two lines made from cones approximately 10 yards apart. (adjust distance if necessary)
Activity:	All the players line up side-by-side behind one of the lines with their balls at their feet. When the coach calls a player's name, that player attempts to kick his ball as close to the opposite line as possible without the ball crossing over the line (over the edge of the

world). The coach must use his personality and get excited as the ball approaches the Edge of the World! The coach can stop the ball just before it goes over. After each player has had a turn, repeat the activity from the other side.

Coaching Considerations:

Fun, challenging, kicking pace and accuracy.

♦ Coordination Exercise 1-2-3-4

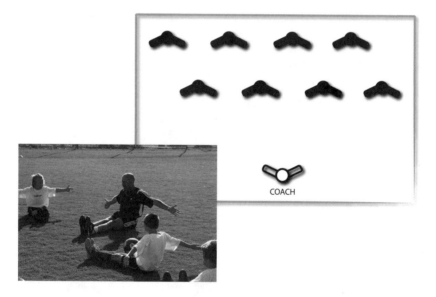

Equipment:	None
Set-up:	Players spread out and sit on the ground in an open area facing the coach, who is also sitting.
Activity:	Coach and players sit with knees pulled into chest and arms around shins. On the count of One, the Coach and players open and straighten their arms wide to the side and extend their straight legs out and together in front; on the count of Two, they close their straight arms by bringing their hands together (clap), while at the same time spreading their straight legs out wide; on the count of Three, everyone resumes position number Two; and on the count of Four, everyone resumes the original starting position

with knees pulled into chest and arms hugging the shins. After practicing the activity slow, try it to the music:

"One-and-a-Two-and-a-Three-and-a-Four!" As they get good at it, have them do two counts of four consecutively to the music. Great Fun!

Coaching Considerations:

Fun, challenging, coordination, decision making.

♦ Soccer Marbles (Hit the Balls)

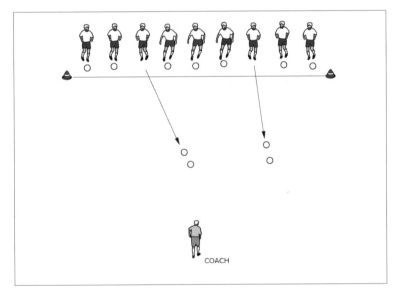

Equipment:	One ball per player. Cones. 2-3 extra soccer balls.
Set-up:	One line made from cones approximately 10-15 yards long. Spread the 2-3 extra soccer balls out in front of the players, about 5-10 yards away.
Activity:	All players line up side-by-side behind the line with their balls at their feet. When the coach calls a player's name, that player attempts to kick his ball and hit one of the extra soccer balls that the coach points to. The player must then quickly retrieve his ball and get back to his position. If they hit the ball, they get 1 point.

Variation:	Players with their soccer balls are positioned on the perimeter of a circle (10 yard radius). Two extra balls are placed in the circle. The coach calls out each players name and the player must try to kick his ball so that it strikes one of the balls in the circle. The player must then quickly retrieve his ball and get back to his position. If a player hits a ball, he gets one point.

Coaching Considerations:

Fun, challenging, kicking pace and accuracy.

◆ Score a Goal (Meg the Coach)

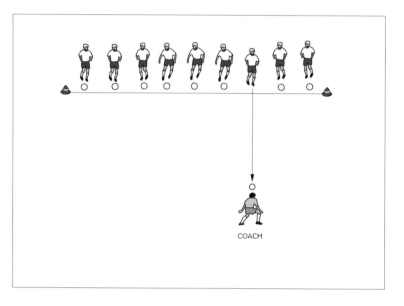

COACH

Equipment:	One ball per player.
Set-up:	One line made from cones approximately 10-15 yards long.
Activity:	All the players line up side-by-side behind the line with their balls at their feet. When the coach calls a player's name, that player attempts to kick his ball through the legs of the coach who is standing, with legs spread, directly in front of the player about 5-10 yards away. The coach makes his way down the line so that every player gets a turn.

Variations: Use 2 cones or 2 flags. The coach simply moves the cones or flags down the line after each player takes his turn.

Coaching Considerations:

Fun, challenging, kicking pace and accuracy.

◆ Controlled Juggling

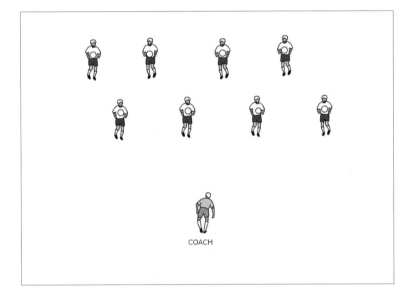

COACH

Equipment: One ball per player.

Set-up: Open area. Players spread out.

Activity: Players start with the ball in their hands. They drop the ball on their thigh (juggle it once), and catch it. As they get better at it, they can try juggling the ball from one thigh to the other thigh and then catch it. The coach can suggest any combination that is reasonable for this age group.

Variations: Foot-catch; thigh-foot-catch; thigh-thigh-foot.

Coaching Considerations:

Fun, hand-thigh-foot-eye coordination, preparation touches.

17

Dynamic Activities

◆ **Line-to-Line Dribbling**

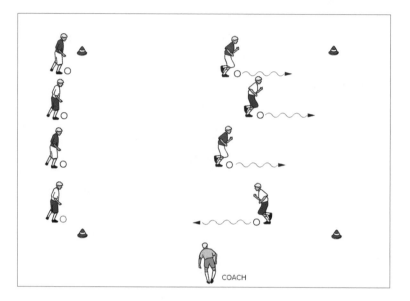

Equipment:	One ball per player. Cones.
Set-up:	Two lines made from cones approximately 20 yards apart. (adjust distance if necessary) Players pair up and form single file lines of two. Pairs line up side-by-side behind one of the cone lines.
Activity:	On the coach's command, the first player in the pair dribbles to the opposite line and returns. When he returns, his partner dribbles to the other line and returns.
Variations:	Tap the ball with the insides of the feet on every touch on the way to the opposite line and back again. Dribble with the inside and outside of the right foot only on the way to the opposite line; dribble with the inside and outside of the left foot only on the way back to your partner.

Coaching Considerations:

Repetitions; proper dribbling mechanics; quick, supple touches; head up.

♦ Dribbling with Moves

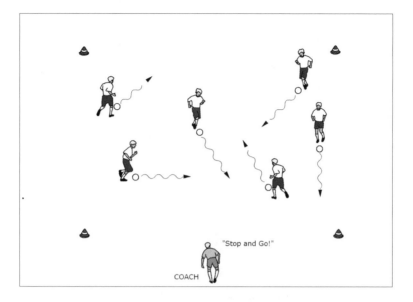

Equipment: One ball per player.

Set-up: Open area or a rectangular grid, approximately 25 yd x 30 yd.

Activity: Players begin by dribbling freely in the proposed area. The coach then introduces the following moves: Stop & Go and Half-turns. After the players practice many repetitions of the moves, they begin to dribble freely once again. The coach then yells out "Stop & Go" or "Half-turn" and the players attempt to perform the move while they are dribbling.

Coaching Considerations:

Movement education, balance, agility, change of speed and direction in order to perform the move.

♦ Interactive Dribbling

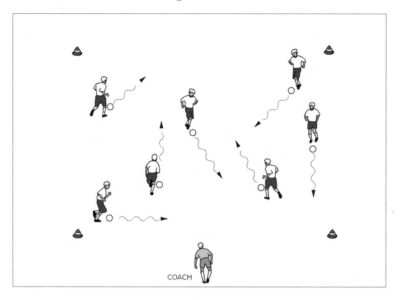

COACH

Equipment: One ball per player.

Set-up: 15 yard x 20 yard rectangular grid.

Activity: All players dribble their soccer balls inside the
                 rectangular grid moving through each other. They try
                 to avoid collisions with other players and their soccer
                 balls.

Variations: On the coach's command (whistle) each player must
                 do a half-turn.
                 On the coach's command (whistle) each player must
                 stop and go.
                 On the coach's command (whistle) each player must
                 fake one way and go the other way.

Coaching Considerations:

                 Fun, dribbling technique, use different surfaces of
                 foot, keep ball close, keep head up, simple decision
                 making.

◆ Fetch (Ball Toss)

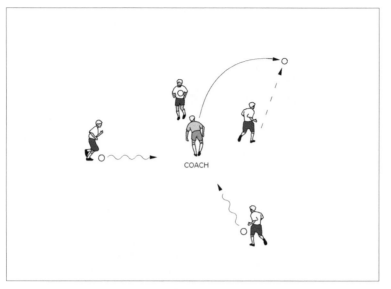

Equipment: One ball per player.

Set-up: Open area; no boundaries.

Activity: Each player holds his ball in his hands. One at a time, each player hands his ball to the coach. The coach then throws (tosses) the ball away from the group, in any direction, and the player proceeds to fetch his ball and bring it back to the coach. This is a very interactive activity, with many players fetching at the same time.

Variations: Players can bring the ball back with their hands, feet, head, thighs, bouncing the ball or rolling the ball on the ground. Use your imagination, but always keep the activity safe.

Coaching Considerations:

Fun, following directions, movement education, hand-eye and foot-eye coordination, simple decision making.

◆ Red Light–Green Light (Stop and Go)

Equipment: One ball per player.

Set-up: Open area, a 10 yard x 15 yard rectangular grid or a circle with radius 10 yards. (Create a playing space appropriate to the age, size and number of players)

Activity: Each player dribbles his ball in any direction. When the coach says, "Red Light", they must stop dribbling and put their foot on the ball. When the coach says, "Green Light", they can dribble again.

Variations:

All players line up side by side at one end. The coach stands just outside of the grid at the other end with his back to the players, so that he cannot see them. When the coach says, "Green Light", all of the players may dribble toward the coach in an effort to cross over the other side of the grid. But, when the coach says, "Red Light", he turns around to make sure each player has stopped dribbling and has put a foot on the ball. If a player is still moving, he must go back to the starting line and play resumes when the coach says, "Green Light".

Coaching Considerations:

Fun, following directions, movement education, dribbling (keeping the ball close), stop and go, simple decision making.

◆ Body Part Dribbling (Stop and Go)

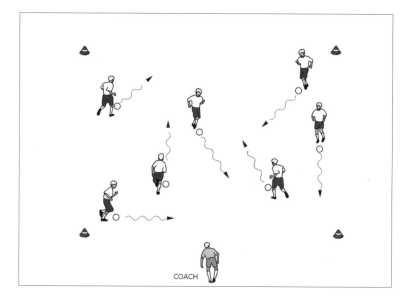

Equipment:	One ball per player.
Set-up:	Open area, a 10 yard x 15 yard rectangular grid or a circle with radius 10 yards. (Create a playing space appropriate to the age, size and number of players)
Activity:	Each player dribbles his ball freely (in any direction). When the coach says, "Stop!", the players can stop the ball with any body part they choose (foot, hand, elbow, etc.). After a short stop, the coach says, "Dribble!" and the players dribble once again. After a few tries, the coach yells out a particular body part instead of the word, "Stop". The players must stop the ball with that particular body part. It really is the game ***Stop and Go*** using a particular body part to stop the ball.

Coaching Considerations:

Fun, following directions, movement education, dribbling, simple decision making.

◆ Musical Soccer Balls

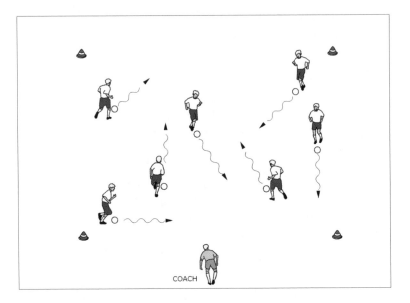

Equipment:	One ball per player.
Set-up:	10 yard x 15 yard rectangular grid or a circle with radius 10 yards. (Create a playing space appropriate to the age, size and number of players)
Activity:	All of the players begin by dribbling their ball freely inside the grid or circle. When the coach begins the music (CD player) or begins to sing, each player must leave his ball and jog around the grid without it. The coach then removes one or two balls from the grid while the music continues. When the music stops, each player tries to retrieve (gain possession of) a ball. The players who do not retrieve a ball must quickly go and get a ball from outside the grid. Then the game begins again.

Coaching Considerations:

Fun, following directions, movement education, simple decision making, anticipation.

◆ Hit the Dirt (Low Flying Airplanes)

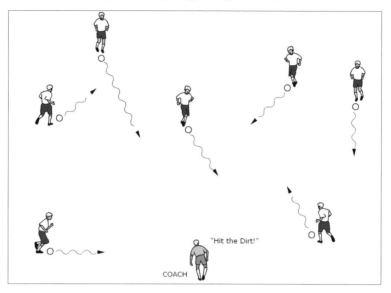

Equipment: One ball per player.

Set-up: Open area, a 10 yard x 15 yard rectangular grid or a circle with radius 10 yards. (Create a playing space appropriate to the age, size and number of players)

Activity: Players dribble freely in all directions. When the coach says, "Hit the Dirt", each player must stop his ball and lie on his chest on the ground. When the coach says, "UP!", each player gets up and begins to dribble freely once again.

Variations:

- When the coach says, "Hit the Dirt!", the players quickly drop down to their chests and jump right back up and continue dribbling.

- Instead of saying "Hit the Dirt!", the coach makes an airplane sound. As the airplane sound gets louder, the players make their own decision when to hit the dirt. As the airplane goes away (sound gets softer), the players get up and dribble freely once again.

Coaching Consideration:

Fun, following directions, movement education (agility, flexibility), simple decision making, anticipation.

25

◆ **Gate Dribbling**

Equipment: One ball per player. Cones.

Set-up: Open area. Gates (2 cones about 1-2 yards apart) are placed at many different angles about 5-10 yards apart. Set up 1 gate per player.

Activity: Players dribble freely through the gates. Once they go through one gate, they must find another gate to dribble through.

Variations:

- Timed gate dribbling...the coach times the players for 30 seconds. The players must count how many gates they dribble through in 30 seconds. Ask players how many they dribbled through when they are finished. Challenge them to increase their score by one on a second attempt.

- Gate Keeper...parents act as gate keepers. They step in between the cones when signaled to do so by the coach. If a parent is in the gate, players cannot dribble through that gate. When the coach signals a parent to step out of the gate, players can dribble through it again.

Coaching Considerations:

Fun, following directions, movement education, dribbling, changing direction, simple decision making (which gate to go through next), anticipation (can I get through that gate before someone else does?).

◆ Cross-Over Dribbling

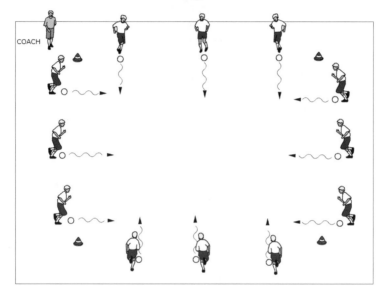

Equipment:	One ball per player.
Set-up:	A 10 yard x 15 yard rectangular grid or a circle with radius 10 yards. (Create a playing space appropriate to the age, size and number of players)
Activity:	If a rectangular grid is being used, set up players, with their balls, on each side of the grid. If a circle is being used, set up players, with their balls, outside the perimeter of the circle. When the coach says, "Green Light" or "Go" or some other key word, the players dribble through the grid or circle to the opposite side. When they reach the opposite side they quickly turn and dribble back to their original spot.

Variations:
- When they reach the opposite side they must return to a place different than their original spot.
- Time the activity to see how many times the players can cross-over in 30 seconds.

- When the coach blows the whistle or yells, "Turn", the players must turn and go in the opposite direction.
- As the players dribble back and forth, the coach can act as a "Bandit" and try to steal a ball or kick it out of the grid. After a few balls are kicked out, the players who have lost their soccer balls become bandits with the coach.

Coaching Considerations:

Fun, following directions, movement education, dribbling, changing direction, simple decision making (how do I make it to the other side without bumping into one of my teammates?), anticipation (what kind of turn will I do when I get to the other side?).

◆ In and Out

Equipment:	One ball per player.
Set-up:	Open area; no boundaries.
Activity:	All of the players dribble their balls through each other **in** a very tight space. When the coach yells, "Get **out** of here!", the players sprint away in any direction, while dribbling their soccer balls. After 3-5 seconds the coach yells, "Come on back **in**!", and the players resume dribbling in the tight space once again.

28

Coaching Considerations:

Fun, following directions, movement education, dribbling, changing direction, speed dribbling or running with the ball, simple decision making (how to avoid bumping into my other teammates), anticipation (when will I have to go fast with the ball?).

◆ Relay Challenge

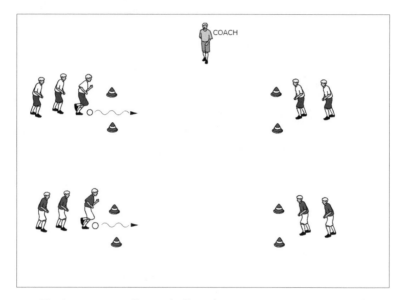

Equipment:	Soccer balls and cones.
Set-up:	Three players in single file line face two other players in single file line ten (10) yards away. The ball is placed with the first player in the line of three. Set up multiple lines so that all players are participating. Adjust the numbers in the lines so that there are at least two relay groups.
Activity:	When the coach says, "Go!", the player with the ball carries it with his hands across to the other line and gives the ball to the first person there. After giving away the ball, he must go to the back of the line. The player who now has the ball must carry it with his hands and run as fast as he can across to the other line and give the ball to the first person there. When the very first player is back in his original spot with ball in hand, the challenge is complete.

- Players bounce the ball.
- Players roll the ball on the ground with their hands.
- Players dribble the ball with their feet.
- Players push the ball on the ground with their head.

Coaching Considerations:

Movement education, hand-eye, foot-eye coordination, dribbling, fun competition (relay races).

◆ Kicking for Distance

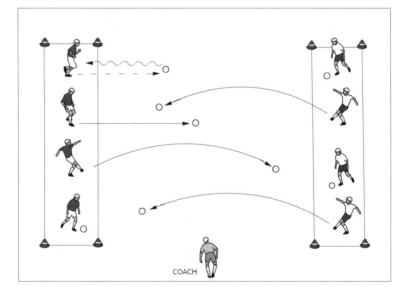

Equipment:	Cones. At least one ball per player.
Set-up:	Rectangular grid approximately 30 yards x 15 yards. Two player zones located at each end of the grid.
Activity:	On the coach's command all players attempt to kick their soccer ball to the opposite end-zone. This is continuous so that all players get many kicking repetitions. When a ball enters their zone from the opposite zone, they can kick it immediately (one-touch) or take a controlling touch and then kick it (2-3 touches).
	If balls stop in the middle zone, any player can run in to retrieve it and bring it back to their end-zone. Kicks can only be taken from the end-zones.

30

Kicking technique: eyes, body shape, foot surface, ball surface, accuracy, pace, non-kicking foot placement, FUN!

♦ Cone Kicking

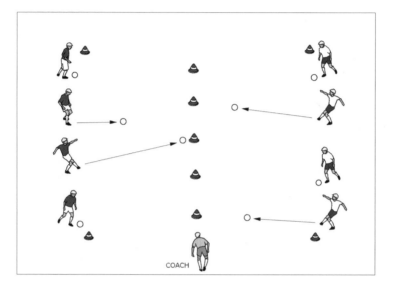

Equipment:	Tall cones, one ball per player.
Set-up:	Rectangular grid approximately 20 yards long x 15 yards wide. Opposing players are positioned at each end of the field outside the rectangular grid. Each player has a ball.
Activity:	On the coach's command, all players attempt to kick their ball and knock down a cone. They receive 1 point for each cone they knock down. Balls will cross over to the opposite side. Once a ball goes past the cones they belong to the opposing team. Players can enter the field to retrieve a ball, but they must be behind the end-line before they can kick a ball.

The game is continuous until all the cones are knocked down. When this happens, the coach calls a time out to set the cones up again and then the game resumes.

Coaching Considerations:

Kicking technique: eyes, body shape, foot surface, ball surface, accuracy, pace, non-kicking foot placement, FUN!

◆ Point Line

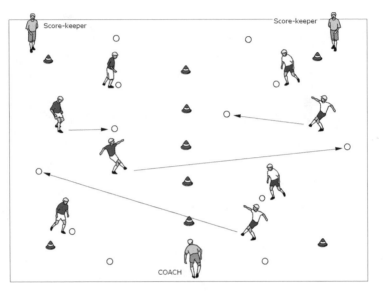

Equipment:	Soccer balls, cones and pinnies.

Set-up: Rectangular grid approximately 30 yards long x 20 yards wide. The midline is marked off by cones. Two teams each positioned in their own half of the field. Each team defends a point line (end-line). Each player is equipped with a ball. Extra balls scattered around the field, on the sides.

The game is played for 3-5 minutes. Multiple games can be played.

Two parents can position themselves at each point line and keep score for the opposite team.

Activity: On the coach's command, players from both teams attempt to kick their soccer balls past the opposing team over the opposing team's point line (end-line). The opposite team can try to stop balls before they cross the line. If a ball crosses the point line, the opposite team gets a point. When this happens, the defending team can retrieve the ball immediately and attempt to kick it over the opposing team's point line.

Coaching Considerations:

Kicking technique: eyes, body shape, foot surface, ball surface, accuracy, pace, distance, non-kicking foot placement, striking moving balls, FUN!

Dynamic Competitive Activities

◆ **Everybody's IT**

Equipment: Cones.

Set-up: 15 yard x 20 yard rectangular grid.

Activity: This is like regular playground "Tag", except every player is **IT**. On the Coach's command every player attempts to tag as many of the other players as possible in 45-60 seconds.

Coaching Considerations:

Fun, following directions, movement education (agility, flexibility), simple decision making, anticipation.

33

♦ Sharks and Minnows

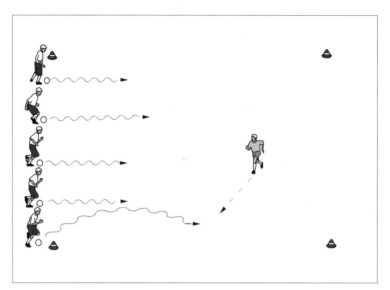

Equipment:	One ball per player and cones.
Set-up:	A 10 yard x 15 yard rectangular grid.
Activity:	All players (minnows) line up side-by-side outside one end of the grid. Each player has a ball at his feet. The Coach (shark) takes a position inside the grid, without a ball, facing the players. When the Coach says, "Swim across to the other side, my little minnows!", all of the minnows (players) attempt to dribble their balls to the opposite side of the grid without getting their ball kicked out of the ocean by the shark. If they make it, they will be able to swim across again and again. If the shark kicks a ball out of the ocean, that minnow turns into a shark and joins the hunt. Once a few minnows become sharks, the coach can step out and facilitate the activity. The last minnow to lose his ball starts the next game as the shark.

Coaching Considerations:

Fun, following directions, movement education, challenging, dribbling, changing speed and direction, speed dribbling or running with the ball, simple decision making (how to avoid the sharks), anticipation (when will I have to go fast with the ball?), defending, tackling.

◆ Cops and Robbers (Knock-Out)

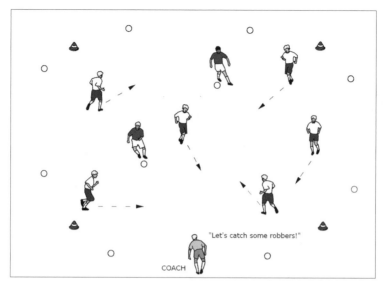

Equipment: Enough balls for all players. Cones.

Set-up: 10 yard x 15 yard rectangular grid. Soccer balls spread around the outside perimeter of the grid.

Activity: All players spread out inside the grid. Only two of them (the Cops) have soccer balls. When the coach says, "Let's catch some Robbers!", The cops attempt to kick their soccer balls at the players who do not have soccer balls (Robbers), who run around in the grid trying to avoid getting hit (caught). *It is extremely important that the Cops kick their soccer balls low so that they hit the Robbers below their knees!* Once a Robber is caught, he "Sees the Light", joins the Police Force, gets a ball from outside the grid and becomes a Cop. The game goes on until all the Robbers have become Cops.

Coaching Considerations:

Fun, following directions, movement education, challenging, dribbling, changing speed and direction, kicking accuracy, simple decision making (how to avoid the cops), anticipation, scheming, agility.

♦ Get Outta' There

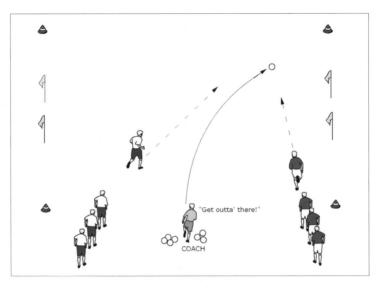

Equipment: Enough balls for all players, cones and flags if available.

Set-up: 15 yard x 20 yard rectangular grid (field). Goals at each end made out of cones or flags, approximately 5-6 steps wide. Coach positioned outside the field at the mid-line with all of the balls. Two teams of players, in different colored pinnies, lined up in single file, on each side of the coach. Goals are designated for each team.

Activity: The coach serves a ball into the field of play. At the moment the ball is played into the field by the coach the first player in each line enters the field and plays 1 v 1 until a goal is scored or the ball goes out of bounds. When that happens, the coach yells, "Get Outta' There!". The players must get off the field quickly and get back in their line. When they are off the field, the coach sends another ball into the field and the next two players enter the field and play 1 v 1. Play continues in this manner until all of the balls are used up. At this point, the coach says that he is out of balls and asks all the players to go get a ball and dribble it back to him.

Variation: The game can be played without goals. Players get a point by dribbling over their designated end-line; players get a point for kicking the ball over their designated end-line.

36

> Fun, challenging, 1 v 1 dribbling (attacking) and tackling (defending) skills, decision making, creativity, scheming.

◆ Boss of the Balls (2 v 2)

Equipment:	Enough balls for all players, cones and flags if available.
Set-up:	15 yard x 20 yard rectangular grid (field). Goals at each end made out of cones or flags, approximately 5-6 steps wide. Coach positioned outside the field at the mid-line with all of the balls. 2 players versus 2 players on the field. Set up two fields so that more of your players are playing.
Activity:	The coach serves a ball into the field of play and play begins. When a ball goes out of bounds or into the goal, the coach sends another ball into the field and play continues in this manner until all the balls are used up. At this point, the coach says that he is out of balls and asks all the players to go get a ball and dribble it back to him.

Coaching Considerations:

> Fun, making decisions that only the game can present, dribbling, shooting, passing, anticipation, excitement.

◆ The Game 3 v 3

Equipment:	Enough soccer balls for all players, cones and flags if available.
Set-up:	15 yard x 20 yard rectangular grid (field). Goals at each end made out of cones or flags, approximately 5-6 steps wide. Coach positioned outside the field at the mid-line with all of the balls. 3 players versus 3 players on the field. Set up two fields so that more of your players are playing.
Activity:	Play 3 v 3 without goalkeepers. Play Boss of the Balls as explained above. The coach serves a ball into the field of play and play begins. When a ball goes out of bounds or into the goal, the coach sends another ball into the field and play continues in this manner until all the balls are used up. At this point, the coach says that he is out of balls and asks all the players to go get a ball and dribble it back to him.

Coaching Considerations:

> Fun, making decisions that only the game can present, dribbling, shooting, passing, anticipation, excitement.

The U8 Age Group

This is the age where players can begin to understand the concept of working with a teammate. The notion, or willingness, to intentionally pass the ball to someone is just beginning to take hold. Coaches and parents will have more success encouraging players to pass the ball in the seven to eight year old age group. In this age group, the player begins to think beyond their personal needs and actively begins to cooperate with a teammate. However, players in this age group must continue individual ball work.

Role of Coach

The role of the coach in the U8 age group is to be a sensitive and patient teacher with an enthusiastic and imaginative approach. It is helpful if they have the ability to demonstrate and very important that they understand technique.

License Requirement

The U6/U8 State Youth Module is required. The National Youth License is recommended.

The U8 Player Characteristics

Mental/Psychological (cognitive)

> Short attention span, but better than U6
> Love to use their imagination…pretend
> Limited ability to attend to more than one task at a time
> Beginning to solve simple soccer problems (i.e. pass to a teammate)
> Some understanding of time and space relations

Physical (psychomotor)

Beginning to develop physical coordination
Improvement in pace regulation
Skeletal system is growing; growth plates near joints
Cardiovascular system is less efficient than an adult's; heart
rate peaks sooner and takes longer to recover
Catching skills are still not developed
Improvement in dribbling and kicking
Love to run, jump, fall and roll

Socially (psychosocial)

Self-concept and body image are beginning to develop
Sensitive...dislike personal failure in front of peers
Negative comments from peers and adults carry great
weight
Limited experience with personal evaluation...effort is
synonymous with successful performance
Inclined more toward cooperative activities (small groups)
Inclined to establish and cooperate with friends
Desire social acceptance; want everyone to like them
Influential person in their life is their father or significant
parent
Like to play soccer because it is FUN; intrinsically
motivated; play for enjoyment

What to Teach U8 Players (Game Components)

Techniques (skills):
Dribbling

With outside of the foot
Change of speed and direction
Moves...scissors, fake one way go the other way

Receiving

> Ground balls with inside, outside, and sole of foot
> Bouncing balls with various body parts
> Ball lifting and juggling

Passing

> With toe, inside of foot and laces
> Throw-ins

Shooting

> With toe, inside of foot and laces

Tackling

> Toe-poke

Catching

> From self and from partner
> Rolling, bouncing, and air balls

Psychology (mental and social):

- Working in pairs
- Sportsmanship
- Dealing with parental involvement
- "How to play" (social cooperation)
- Emotional management

Fitness (movement education):

- Introduce the idea of warm-up
- Agility
- Leaping
- Tumbling
- Eye/foot & eye/hand coordination

Tactics (decisions):

- Being exposed to all positions
- 1 v 1 attacking
- 1 v 1 defending
- 2 v 1 attacking
- Introduce the names of positions
- Shape (triangles, diamond, box)

Rules:

        Review the kick off
        Review the goal kick
        Review hand ball
        Review physical fouls (pushing, holding, striking, tripping)
        The corner kick
        Direct kicks
        Throw-ins

US Youth Soccer Modifications to The Game

Playing numbers: 4 v 4 (no goalkeepers)
Field Dimensions:
     Length   25-35 yards
     Width   20-30 yards
Goal Dimensions:
     Height   6 feet
     Width   18 feet
Duration: four 12-minute quarters
Ball: number 3

Possible Formations

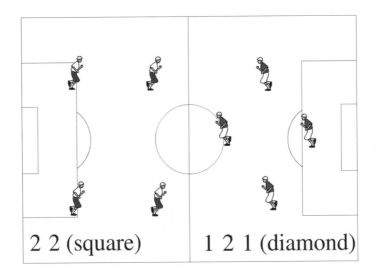

2 2 (square)   1 2 1 (diamond)

The Training Session

General Information

- ✓ The training session should involve fun and imaginative game like activities.
- ✓ Light coaching on simple technique is appropriate (dribbling, passing and receiving)
- ✓ Small-sided directional games such as 1 v 1, 2 v 1, 2 v 2, 3v2, and 3 v 3 should be included as well. Simple explanations regarding shape and positions.
- ✓ Training should always conclude with a 4 v 4 game without goalkeepers.
- ✓ The duration of the training session should be 60-75 minutes.

Lesson Plan Design

The U8 training session should consist of about 6-8 activities. There should be a mixture of dynamic, relaxation and dynamic competitive activities. The design would be as follows:

1. Dynamic Activity
2. Dynamic Activity
3. Dynamic Activity
4. Relaxation Activity
5. Dynamic Competitive Activity
6. Dynamic Competitive Activity

Sample Lesson Plan

1. Interactive Dribbling
2. Math Dribble
3. Hit the Dirt
4. Croquet
5. Get Outta' There
6. The Game 4 v 4

U8 Training Activities Table

Relaxation	Dynamic	Dynamic Competitive
Coach "Tom" Says (Simon Says)	Fetch (Ball Toss in 2's and 3's)	Tag with a Pinnie
Do This-Do That	Interactive Dribbling	Combat
Croquet	Math Dribble	Sharks and Minnows
Bounce Juggling	Hit the Dirt	Bandit Ball (Keep your ball)
Controlled Juggling	Gate Dribbling (Gate Keepers)	Directional 2 v 1
	Relay Challenge	Directional 3v2
	Circle Passing	Four Corner Shooting
	Passing in Two's (2's)	Get Outta' There by the Numbers
	Gate Passing in Two's (2's)	Boss of the Balls (3 v 3 or 4 v 4)
	Kicking for Distance	The Game 4 v 4
	Cone Kicking	
	Point Line	
	Serve-to-Self Receiving	

__Use any of the U6 activities that you feel are appropriate and fun for the players.__

U8 Training Activities

Relaxation Activities

♦ Coach "Tom" Says (Simon Says)

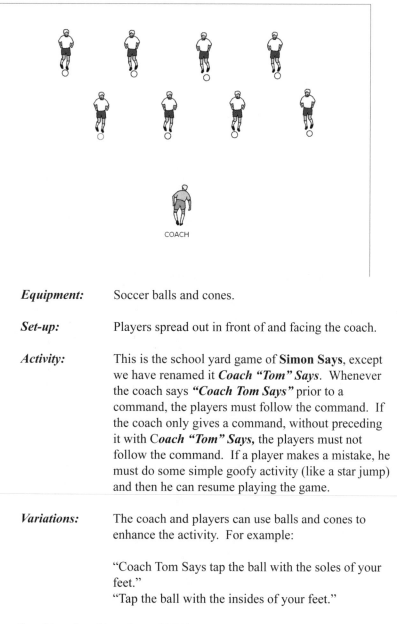

Equipment:	Soccer balls and cones.
Set-up:	Players spread out in front of and facing the coach.
Activity:	This is the school yard game of **Simon Says**, except we have renamed it *Coach "Tom" Says*. Whenever the coach says *"Coach Tom Says"* prior to a command, the players must follow the command. If the coach only gives a command, without preceding it with *Coach "Tom" Says,* the players must not follow the command. If a player makes a mistake, he must do some simple goofy activity (like a star jump) and then he can resume playing the game.
Variations:	The coach and players can use balls and cones to enhance the activity. For example:
	"Coach Tom Says tap the ball with the soles of your feet." "Tap the ball with the insides of your feet."

Coaching Considerations: FUN!

♦ Do This-Do That

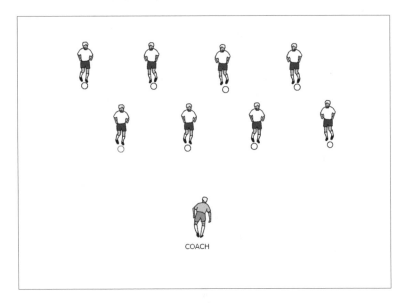

COACH

Equipment:	Soccer balls and cones.
Set-up:	Players spread out in front of and facing the coach.
Activity:	This is the school yard game of **Simon Says**, except we have renamed it to **Do This–Do That**. Whenever the coach says, *"Do This"*, prior to a simple command, the players must follow the command. Whenever the coach says, *"Do That"*, prior to a simple command, the players must NOT follow the command. If a player makes a mistake, he must do some simple goofy activity (like a star jump) and then he can resume playing the game.
Variations:	The coach and players can use soccer balls and cones to enhance the activity.

♦ Croquet

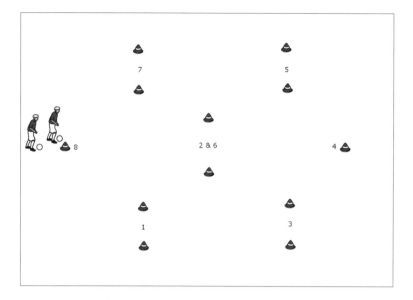

Equipment: Soccer balls and cones.

Set-up: Set up multiple croquet fields with cones instead of wickets. Adjust distances between cones so that it is appropriate for using soccer balls and it is challenging to the players.

Activity: Each player plays against one opponent. One of the players starts the game by kicking his ball in the direction of wicket (gate) #1. Players alternate turns. (A turn is one kick of the ball)

The object of the game is to get from start to finish before your opponent does. You do this by kicking your ball through the front of wickets 1, 2 and 3; then kicking your ball so that it hits cone #4; then kicking your ball through wickets 5, 6 and 7; and finally kicking your ball so that it hits cone #8. Each time you successfully kick your ball through a wicket, you get an additional turn. If your opponent hits your ball with his ball, you must go back to the beginning and start all over again.

Coaching Considerations: Passing accuracy and pace, FUN!

◆ Bounce Juggling

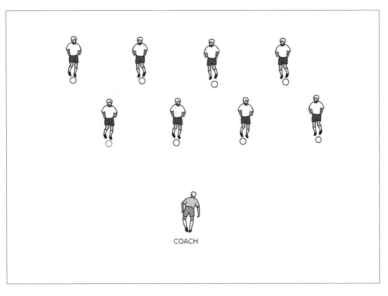

Equipment: One ball per player.

Set-up: Open area. Players spread out.

Activity: Players start with the soccer ball in their hands or at their feet.
They attempt to keep the ball in the air using their feet, thighs and head (juggling). The ball can bounce in between touches.

Coaching Considerations:

Fun, hand-thigh-foot-eye coordination, preparation touches.

◆ Controlled Juggling

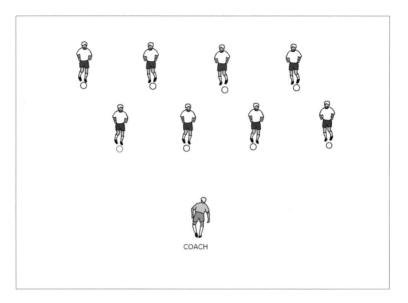

Equipment: One ball per player.

Set-up: Open area. Players spread out.

Activity: Players start with the soccer ball in their hands or at
their feet.
The coach asks them to do specific juggling
sequences:

Foot-Foot-Catch
Thigh-Thigh-Foot-Catch
Thigh-Thigh-Head-Catch
Thigh-Foot-Head-Catch

Coaching Considerations:

Fun, hand-thigh-foot-eye coordination, preparation
touches.

Dynamic Activities

◆ Fetch (Ball Toss in 2's and 3's)

Equipment:	One ball for 2 players or 3 players.
Set-up:	Open area; no boundaries.
Activity:	One of the players in each group holds the ball in his hands. One at a time, each player hands his ball to the coach. The coach then throws the ball away from the group, in any direction, and the group of players proceeds to fetch their ball and bring it back to the coach. This is a very interactive, cooperative activity, with many groups of players fetching their ball at the same time.
Variations:	The groups of players can bring the ball back with:

- Two left hands.
- A foot and a hand.
- Three hands.
- Two foreheads.
- Only four passes.

Coaching Considerations:

Fun, following directions, movement education, hand-eye and foot-eye coordination, simple decision making, cooperation.

◆ Interactive Dribbling

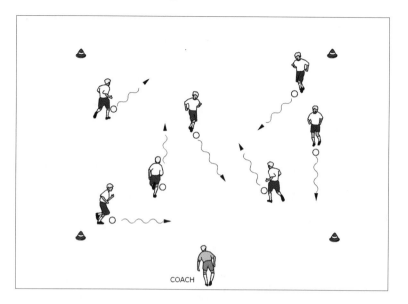

Equipment:	One ball per player.
Set-up:	15 yard x 20 yard rectangular grid.
Activity:	All players dribble their soccer balls inside the rectangular grid moving through each other. They try to avoid collisions with other players and their balls.
Variations:	On the coach's command (whistle) each player must do a half-turn. On the coach's command (whistle) each player must stop and go. On the coach's command (whistle) each player must fake one way and go the other way.

Coaching Considerations:

Fun, dribbling technique, use different surfaces of foot, keep ball close, keep head up, simple decision making.

◆ Math Dribble

Equipment:	One ball per player.
Set-up:	Open area; no boundaries.
Activity:	All players dribble interactively. When the coach shouts out a number, the players must quickly get into a group with that number of players in it. For example, if the coach shouts out, "Three!" the players must form groups of three as fast as they can. If some of the players were unable to form a group of three, as in this example, they would do some kind of goofy exercise (i.e. star jump, etc.).
Variations:	The coach can shout:

Two plus two.
Two plus one.
One times two.

Coaching Considerations: Dribbling technique, cooperation, listening, anticipation, math skills, FUN!

◆ Hit the Dirt

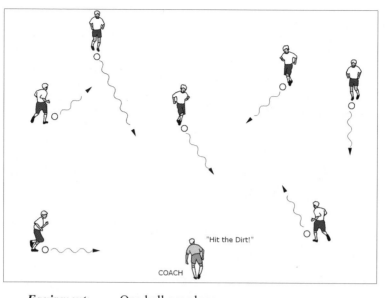

Equipment: One ball per player.

Set-up: 10 yd x 15 yd rectangular grid or a circle with a 10 yard radius or an open area. (Create a playing space appropriate to the age, size and number of players)

Activity: Players dribble freely in all directions. When the coach shouts, "Hit the Dirt!" players must stop their balls and lie on their chest on the ground. When the coach says , "Up!" the players get up and begin to dribble freely once again.

Variations: When the player hits the dirt, he must perform a log roll before getting back up to his feet.

The player must get down to the ground and back on his feet before his ball stops moving.

The player must perform a half turn when he returns to his feet and get possession of his ball.

Coaching Considerations:

Fun, following directions, movement education (agility and flexibility), dribbling (keeping the ball close), stop and go, simple decision making, anticipation. Refer to U6 Activities.

◆ Gate Dribbling (Gate Keepers)

Equipment: One ball per player. Cones.

Set-up: Open area. Gates (2 cones about 1-2 yards apart) are placed at many different angles about 5-10 yards apart. Set up 1 gate per player or 1 more gate than there are players (i.e. 6 or 7 gates for 6 players).

Activity: Players dribble freely through the gates. Once they go through one gate, they must find a different gate to dribble through.

Ask parents to be Gate Keepers. Each Gate keeper stands next to a gate. When the coach looks at a Gate Keeper, he must get inside the gate. When a Gate Keeper is inside the gate, players cannot dribble through it. When a Gate Keeper moves outside of the gate, players are free to dribble through the gate. Each time the coach looks at a Gate Keeper, the Gate Keeper simply moves in or out of the gate.

Variations: Timed gate dribbling with Gate Keepers...the coach times the players for 30 seconds. The players must count how many gates they dribble through in 30 seconds. This is funny because they really can't count and concentrate on dribbling at the same time. When time is up ask the group a question like: "Did everybody go through 5 gates?" This will stimulate a fun discussion with the players because they will want to brag about how many gates they went through.

Coaching considerations:

Fun, following directions, movement education, dribbling, changing direction, simple decision making (which gate to go through next?) anticipation (can I get through that gate before a Gate Keeper gets in?).

◆ Relay Challenge

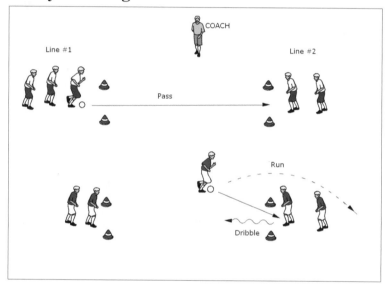

Equipment: Soccer balls and cones.

Set-up: Three players in single file line face two other players in single file line ten (10) yards away. The ball is placed with the first player in the line of three. Set up multiple lines so that all players are participating.

Adjust the numbers in the lines so that there are at least two or three relay groups.

The coach can reduce the number of players in each relay group so that players can get more touches and the pace is faster. Minimum of 3 players in a relay group (2 payers facing one player).

Activity: **Pass-Receive-Dribble**...First player in line #1 passes the ball to the first player in line #2. After he passes the ball, he must run to the back of line #2. The player receiving the ball must control it and dribble to line #1, giving the ball to the first person in that line, and then going to the back of the line. The sequence continues in this manner.

Variations: **Serve-Control-Pass**... First player in line #1 serves (with his hands) a bouncing ball to the first player in line #2. After he serves the ball, he must run to the back of line #2. The player receiving the ball must control it and pass it to the first person in line #1, follow the pass and go to the end of line #1. The sequence continues in this manner.

Coaching Considerations: Dribbling technique (keeping the ball close); proper preparation touch; passing accuracy and appropriate pace.

◆ Circle Passing

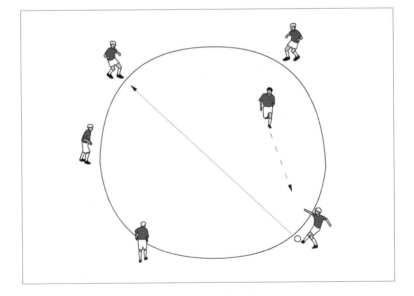

Equipment: 2 soccer balls.

Set-up: All the players position themselves around the center circle. One player has the ball to begin the activity.

Activity: The player with the ball passes to another player
(it cannot be a player next to him), follows his pass
and replaces the player he passed to. The player
receiving the pass has two touches to control and
pass the ball to someone else on the circle. He then
follows his pass and replaces that player on the circle.
This continues until the ball is played outside of the
circle. Use Time as a challenge to the players…they
must keep the ball moving, with the appropriate
touches, inside the circle for one minute!

Variations:

- One touch only using one ball..
- Use 2 balls. Keep both balls moving for a
  timed period.

Coaching Considerations:

Intelligent movement, head up, preparing to receive
the ball, surveying the area, looking for their target
early, anticipation, passing accuracy and pace,
communication.

◆ Passing in Two's (2's)

Equipment:	One ball for two players (pair).
Set-up:	Open area.
Activity:	Each pair passes their ball on the ground to each other freely. They must keep their feet and the ball moving. They remain in a specified area. They can 1-touch the ball (pass immediately without controlling the ball) or 2-touch the ball (take one controlling touch before passing the ball).
Variations:	Passing competition – when the coach says, "GO!" each pair counts how many passes they can complete in a specified time (30-60 seconds).

◆ Gate Passing in Two's (2's)

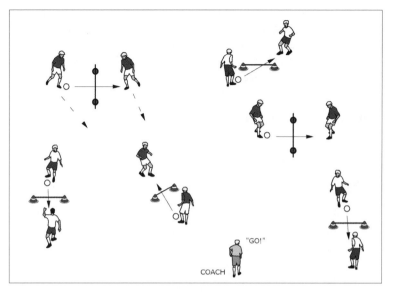

Equipment: One ball for two players (pair). 20-30 cones.

Set-up: Open area. Gates (2 cones about 1-2 yards apart) are placed at many different angles about 10 yards apart. Set up one gate per pair or 1 more gate than there are pairs. (i.e. 5-6 gates for 5 pairs)

Activity: Each pair passes their ball to each other freely through the gates. Once they pass their ball through one gate, they must find another gate to pass through.

Variations:

- Timed gate passing…the coach times the players for 30 seconds. The players must count how many gates they pass their ball through in 30 seconds. Ask each pair how many gates they passed their ball through when they are finished. Challenge them to increase their score by one on a second attempt.

- Gate Keeper…parents act as gate keepers. They step in between the cones of a gate when signaled to do so by the coach. If a parent is in the gate, players cannot pass their ball through that gate. When the coach signals a parent to step out of the gate, players can pass through it again.

Fun, passing and dribbling, changing direction, simple
decision making (which gate to go through next), timing
(when and how hard should I pass the ball to my partner),
anticipation (can I pass my ball through that gate before
someone else does?).

♦ Kicking for Distance

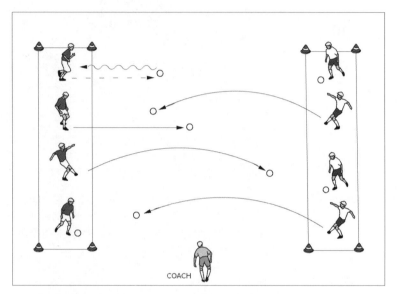

Equipment:	Cones. At least one ball per player.
Set-up:	Rectangular grid approximately 35 yards x 20 yards. Two player zones located at each end of the grid.
Activity:	On the coach's command all players attempt to kick their ball to the opposite end-zone. This is continuous so that all players get many kicking repetitions. When a ball enters their zone from the opposite zone, they can kick it immediately (one-touch) or take a controlling touch and then kick it (2-3 touches).
	If balls stop in the middle zone, any player can run in to retrieve it and bring it back to their end-zone. Kicks can only be taken from the end-zones.

Kicking technique: eyes, body shape, foot surface, ball surface, accuracy, pace, non-kicking foot placement, FUN!

◆ Cone Kicking

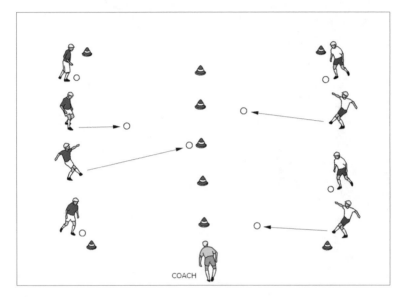

Equipment:	Tall cones, one ball per player.
Set-up:	Rectangular grid approximately 30 yards long x 25 yards wide. Opposing players are positioned at each end of the field outside the rectangular grid. Each player has a ball.
Activity:	On the coach's command, all players attempt to kick their ball and knock down a cone. They receive 1 point for each cone they knock down. Balls will cross over to the opposite side. Once a ball goes past the cones they belong to the opposing team. Players can enter the field to retrieve a ball, but they must be behind the end-line before they can kick a ball.

The game is continuous until all the cones are knocked down. When this happens, the coach calls a time out to set the cones up again and then the game resumes.

Kicking technique: eyes, body shape, foot surface, ball surface, accuracy, pace, non-kicking foot placement, FUN!

♦ Point Line

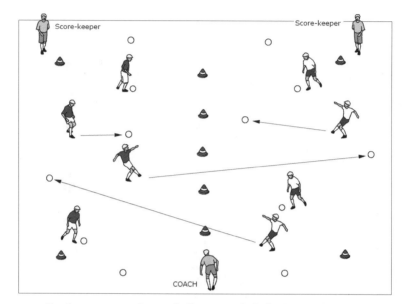

Equipment:	Soccer balls, cones and pinnies.
Set-up:	Rectangular grid approximately 40 yards long x 25 yards wide. The midline is marked off by cones. Two teams each positioned in their own half of the field. Each team defends a point line (end-line). Each player is equipped with a soccer ball. Extra balls scattered around the field, on the sides.
	The game is played for 3-5 minutes. Multiple games can be played.
	Two parents can position themselves at each point line and keep score for the opposite team.
Activity:	On the coach's command, players from both teams attempt to kick their balls past the opposing team over the opposing team's point line (end-line). The opposite team can try to stop balls before they cross the line. If a ball crosses the point line, the opposite team gets a point. When this happens, the defending

team can retrieve the ball immediately and attempt to kick it over the opposing team's point line.

Coaching Considerations:

Kicking technique: eyes, body shape, foot surface, ball surface, accuracy, pace, distance, non-kicking foot placement, striking moving balls, FUN!

◆ Serve-to-Self Receiving

Equipment:	One ball per player.
Set-up:	25 yard x 30 yard rectangular grid.
Activity:	All players dribble their balls inside the rectangular grid moving through each other. They try to avoid collisions with other players and their balls. When the coach yells, "Laces", each player picks up his ball and serves it in the air to himself. They attempt to receive the ball with their "Laces" before it touches the ground. Once they have cushioned the ball to the ground, they continue to dribble around in the area. The coach can vary the command such as "Thigh" or "Chest" to promote other receiving surfaces.

> Fun, receiving air balls with the laces, thighs and chest; getting to the ball in the air; comfort with the ball in the air; providing receiving surfaces for the ball; cushioning the ball; keeping the ball within dribbling distance.

Dynamic Competitive Activities

♦ **Tag with Pinnie**

Equipment:	Cones and pinnies.
Set-up:	15 yard x 20 yard rectangular grid.
Activity:	This is regular playground "Tag". The coach selects one or two players to be **IT**. They are equipped with a pinnie that they hold in their hand. Their job is to tag another player. When they tag another player, they are no longer **IT** so they drop their pinnie and the person they tagged picks it up and becomes a new **IT**. Play for 45-60 seconds. Select some new **IT's** and play again.

Variations:

- **IT's** don't have a ball while everyone else is dribbling a ball.
- Everyone is dribbling a ball, including the **IT's**.

Coaching Considerations: Agility, flexibility, speed, scheming, FUN!

◆ Combat

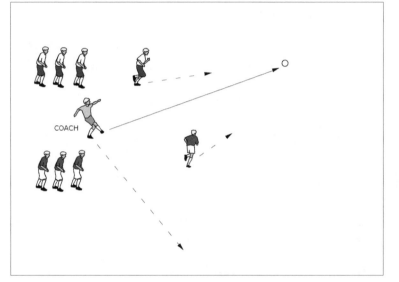

Equipment: One ball. Scrimmage vests in two colors.

Set-up: Open area; no boundaries. Coach equipped with the soccer ball. Color-coded players lined up in two single file lines; one line on the right side of the coach and one line on the left side of the coach facing toward the open area.

Activity: When the coach kicks the ball out into the open area, the first player in each line attempts to get to the ball, keep possession of the ball and get it back to the coach, while the other player is defending him, trying to gain possession himself. The player that gets the ball back to the coach gets a point. This is a 1 v 1 duel in open space. The moment the coach gets the ball back, he kicks it out again for the next players in each line.

After the coach kicks out the ball, he should move away from the other players. There are two reasons for this. One…risk to the other players. Two…the players in the competition will look back for their target, anticipating how to turn on their opponent.

Variations: If, before the coach kicks the ball out, he says, "Two!", then 2 players from each line chase the ball and we have a 2 v 2 competition. The coach can manipulate the activity by calling out, "Three!" or "Four!".

Coaching Considerations:

1 v 1 attacking and defending skills and decision making, dribbling , shielding, tackling.

♦   **Sharks and Minnows**

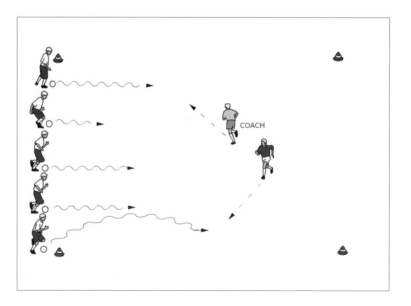

Equipment: One ball per player. Cones.

Set-up: 10 yard x 15 yard rectangular grid. All players (minnows) line up side-by-side outside one end of the grid. Each player has a ball at his feet. The Coach (shark) takes a position inside the grid, without a ball, facing the players.

| *Activity:* | When the Coach says, "Swim across to the other side, my little minnows!", all of the minnows (players) attempt to dribble their balls to the opposite side of the grid without getting it kicked out of the ocean by the shark (coach). If they make it, they will be able to swim across again and again. If the shark kicks a ball out of the ocean, that minnow turns into a shark and joins the other shark. Once a few minnows become sharks, the coach can step out and facilitate the activity. The last minnow to lose his ball will start the next game as the shark. |

Coaching Considerations:

Fun, following directions, movement education, challenging, dribbling, changing speed and direction, speed dribbling or running with the ball, simple decision making (how to avoid the sharks), anticipation (when will I have to go fast with the ball?).

♦ Bandit Ball (Keep your ball)

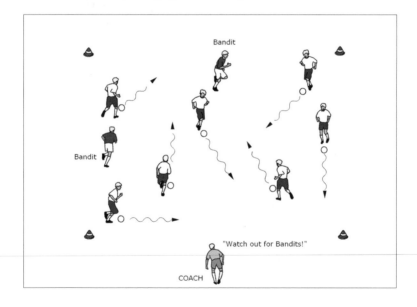

| *Equipment:* | One ball per player and cones. |
| *Set-up:* | A 10 yard x 15 yard rectangular grid. 30-45 second games. |

Activity: All players are dribbling their balls inside the grid, with the exception of one or two players, who do not have balls (the bandits). When the coach says, "Watch out for bandits!", the bandits try to steal someone's ball. Once they have stolen a ball, they dribble it and try to keep possession of it; they are no longer a bandit. If a player loses a ball, he becomes a bandit and attempts to steal a ball. If a ball is kicked out of the grid, it cannot be brought back in. Start each game with new bandits. At the end of each game one point is awarded to the players who have possession of a ball.

Coaching Considerations:

Dribbling, individual possession (keeping the ball), constructive tackling (winning the ball), decision making, scheming.

◆ Directional 2 v 1

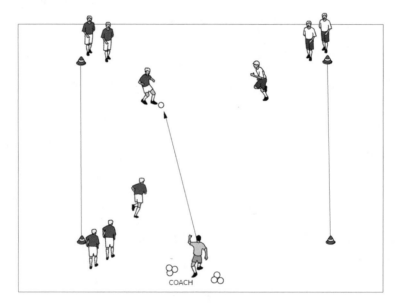

Equipment: Soccer balls, cones and pinnies.

Set-up: Rectangular grid 20 yards x 15 yards. Separate players into 3 lines positioned as in the diagram. Two attacker lines and one defender line.

Activity:	The Coach passes a ball to one of the lines. The 1st player in each of the three lines enters the field. This creates a 2 v 1 situation. The two attackers must get the ball over the opposite end-line under control. If they do this, they are awarded 1 point. If the defender wins possession of the ball and gets the ball over the opposite end-line, he is awarded 2 points. If the ball goes out of bounds or points are scored, the coach serves another ball in and new players enter the field.
Variations:	This game can be played to zones or goals.

Coaching Considerations:

Dribbling, passing, receiving, combination play, defending (delay, intercepting passes).

♦ Directional 3v2

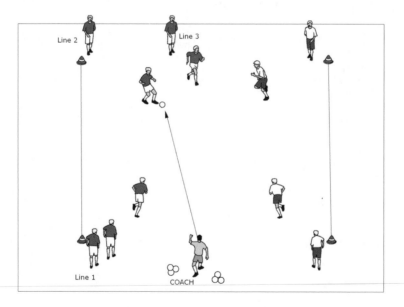

Equipment:	Soccer balls, cones and pinnies.
Set-up:	Rectangular grid 30 yards x 20 yards. Separate players into 5 lines positioned as in the diagram. Three attacker lines and two defender lines.

Activity: The Coach passes a ball to one of the lines. The 1st
                   player in each of the five lines enters the field. This
                   creates a 3v2 situation. The three attackers must get
                   the ball over the opposite end-line under control.
                   If they do this, they are awarded 1 point. If the
                   defenders win possession of the ball and get the ball
                   over the opposite end-line, they are awarded 2 points.
                   If the ball goes out of bounds or points are scored, the
                   coach serves another ball in and new players enter the
                   field.

Variations: This game can be played to zones or goals.

Coaching Considerations:

                   Dribbling, passing, receiving, combination play,
                   defending (delay, intercepting passes).

◆ Four Corner Shooting

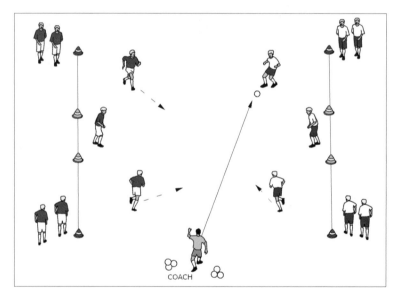

Equipment: Enough balls for all players, pinnies, goals, cones and
                   flags if available.

Set-up: 25 yard x 30 yard rectangular grid (field). Goals at
                   each end of the field. Coach positioned outside the
                   field at the mid-line with all of the balls. Two teams

of players, in different colored pinnies; half of each team lined up in single file behind a specified corner cone (4 lines); one team at one end and one team at the other end. Goals are designated for each team and goalkeepers are positioned in each goal.

Activity: When the coach serves a ball into the field of play, the first player in each of the four lines enters the field and a 3 v 3 competition begins (2 field players and a goalkeeper for each team). Play continues until a goal is scored or the ball goes out of bounds. When this happens, the players must get off the field quickly and get back in their line. When they are off the field, the coach sends another ball into the field, and the competition continues with the next players in each line. Play continues in this manner until all of the balls are used up. At this point, the coach says that he is out of balls and asks all the players to go get a ball and dribble it back to him. Once the balls are collected, a new round of play begins.

Variations: Make the field a bit larger, 30 yards wide x 35 yards long. Now when the coach serves the ball into the field of play, two players from each of the four lines enter the field and a 5 v 5 competition begins (includes goalkeepers).

Coaching Considerations:

Technique under the pressure of a game, decision making in the competitive game environment, triangular shape, passing and receiving, shooting, FUN!

◆ Get Outta' There by the Numbers

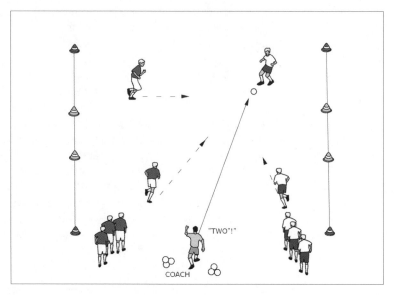

Equipment:	Enough balls for all players, pinnies, cones and flags if available.
Set-up:	15 yard x 20 yard rectangular grid (field). Goals at each end made out of cones or flags, approximately 5-6 steps wide. Coach positioned outside the field at the mid-line with all of the balls. Two teams of players, in different colored pinnies, lined up in single file, on each side of the coach. Goals are designated for each team.
Activity:	The coach serves a ball into the field of play. If the coach shouts, "One!", just before he serves the ball in the first player in each line enters the field and plays 1 v 1 until a goal is scored or the ball goes out of bounds. If the coach shouts "Two!" just before he serves the ball in, two players from each line enter the field and play 2 v 2 until a goal is scored or the ball goes out of bounds. When this happens, the coach yells,"Get Outta' There!". The players must get off the field quickly and get back in their line. When they are off the field, the coach shouts out a number and sends another ball into the field, and the competition begins. Play continues in this manner until all of the balls are used up. At this point, the coach says that he is out of balls and asks all the players to go get a ball and dribble it back to him.

Variation:	If the coach shouts, "Yellow!", just before he serves the ball in, two players from the yellow line (team) and only one player from the red line (team) enter the field and play 2 v 1 until a goal is scored or the ball goes out of bounds.
	Another option might be…if the coach shouts, "Red!", just before he serves the ball in, three players from the red line (team) and only two players from the yellow line (team) enter the field and play 3 v 2 until a goal is scored or the ball goes out of bounds.

Coaching Considerations:

Fun, challenging, dribbling and passing (attacking) and tackling (defending) skills, decision making, simple combination play, creativity, scheming. Playing with even and uneven numbers on the field.

◆ Boss of the Balls (3 v 3 or 4 v 4)

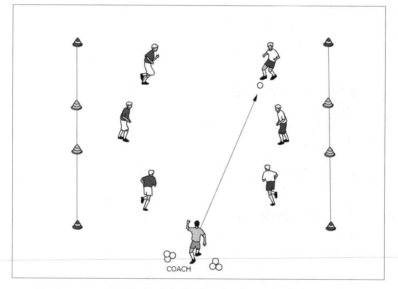

Equipment:	Enough balls for all players, cones and flags
Set-up:	15 yard x 20 yard rectangular grid (field). Adjust field size if necessary. Goals at each end made out of cones or flags, approximately 5-6 steps wide. Coach positioned outside the field at the mid-line with all of the balls. 3 v 3 or 4 v 4 on the field.

Activity: The coach serves a ball into the field of play and play begins. When a ball goes out of bounds or into the goal, the coach sends another ball into the field and play continues in this manner until all the balls are used up. At this point, the coach says that he is out of balls and asks all the players to go get a ball and dribble it back to him.

Coaching Considerations:

Fun, making decisions that only the game can present, dribbling, shooting, passing, anticipation, excitement.

♦ The Game 4 v 4

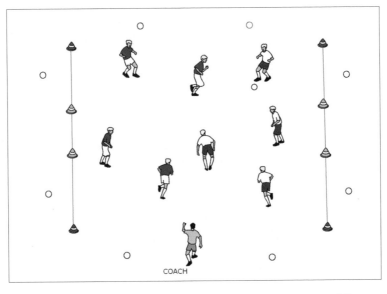

Equipment: Enough balls for all players. Cones and flags if available.

Set-up: 20 yard x 25 yard rectangular grid (field). Goals at each end made out of cones or flags, approximately 5-6 steps wide. Balls are placed outside and around the field. 4 v 4 on the field. Set up two fields so that more of your players are playing.

Activity: One of the players on one of the teams starts play by kicking a ball to the other team. From that point on the game is continuous. US Youth Soccer modified rules are used.

Variations: When a ball goes out of play, the coach serves
                   another one in until all the balls are gone (like Boss
                   of the Balls).

Coaching Considerations:

                   Fun, making decisions that only the game can
                   present, dribbling, shooting, passing, rectangular/
                   diamond shape, anticipation, excitement.

The U10 Age Group

The motivation to learn basic skills is very high at this age level. Children gradually begin to change from being self-centered to being self-critical and develop the need for group and/or team games. The game itself should be central to all skills training. Small-sided games continue to be the method of choice for this age group. This is an appropriate time to introduce some of the basic _**Principles**_ of play which are shown in bold below:

Attacking Principles	_Defensive Principles_
**Penetration**	_**Recovery (Immediate Chase)**_
**Support**	_**Pressure**_
Mobility	_**Cover**_
Width	Balance
Depth (length)	Compactness
**Improvisation (deception, creativity)**	Counter Attack

For more information on attacking and defensive principles please refer to Tactics page 173-177.

Role of Coach

The role of the coach in the U10 age group is to be a patient and motivating teacher. At this level, in addition to understanding technique, coaches should be able to provide environments conducive to problem solving (decision-making) by the players utilizing guided discovery methods.

License Requirement

The U10/U12 State Youth Module is required. The National Youth License is recommended.

The U10 Player Characteristics

Mental/Psychological (cognitive)

Lengthened attention span
Ability to sequence thought and actions; begin to think in advance of the ball…anticipate
Ability to remember, follow more complex instructions and solve higher-level problems (i.e. simple combination play)
Developing ability to focus and stay on task
More understanding of time and space relations

Physical (psychomotor)

Gain a tremendous amount of physical strength, endurance and power; this is related to body size and muscle mass
Motor performance includes a variety of motor tasks that require speed, balance, flexibility, explosive strength and muscular endurance; pace factor is developing quite well
Gross and small fine motor skills becoming refined
Children this age are in a linear growth mode (head to toe)
Height can approach 5 feet and weight can approach 80 lbs

Socially (psychosocial)

Self-concept and body image are important
Less Sensitive…but still dislike personal failure in front of peers
Begin to initiate play on their own…they want to play
Becoming more serious about their play
Inclined more toward small group and team activities
Peer group attachment and pressure becoming significant
Adults outside the family become influential (coach, teacher, etc.)
Gender differences becoming more apparent

What to Teach U10 Players (Game Components)

Techniques (skills):

Running with the Ball
At speed

Under Pressure

Passing
With outside of the foot
Heading

Instep Drive
Shooting

Crossing

Receiving Ground Balls with the Inside and Outside of Foot
Away from pressure
Past opponent

Receiving Air Balls
With the Instep (cushion) and sole, inside and outside of the foot (wedge)

Throw-In
Short and long distances

Moves in Dribbling
Rolls, scissors-push, double scissors, step-over chop

Introduce Heading
Juggling (alone and in small groups)
Feet in contact with the ground

Introduction to jumping

Tackling
Balance foot and contact foot (block tackle)

Goalkeeping (skills)
Ready Stance for Goalkeepers

Foot positioning

Body posture
"W" Grip

Positioning of thumbs

Fingers spread
How to Hold a Ball After a Save
Ball to chest

Forearm protection
Catching Shots at the Keeper
Body alignment path of ball
Punting

Distance and accuracy
Throwing

Bowling

Over-arm
Goal Kicks
Distance and accuracy

Psychology (mental and social):
- Working in groups of 3-6
- Staying focused for one entire half
- Sensitivity; learning how to win, lose or draw gracefully
- Sportsmanship
- How to handle parental involvement
- Communication; emotional management

Fitness (conditioning):
- Endurance
- Range of motion-flexibility
- Proper warm-up is now mandatory
- Introduce cool-down

Tactics (decisions):
- Roles of 1st attacker and defender
- Roles of 2nd attackers and defenders

- 2 v 1 attacking (simple combinations)
- Man-to-man defending
- Throw-ins to teammate's feet
- Introduction to the tactics of set plays/restarts (goal kicks, corner kicks, other free kicks)
- Introduction to setting up walls

Rules:

Review Fouls and Misconduct

US Youth Soccer Modifications to The Game

Playing numbers: 6v6 (with goalkeepers)
Field Dimensions:
    Length   45-60 yards
    Width   35-45 yards
Goal Dimensions:
    Height   6 feet
    Width   18 feet
Duration: two periods of 25 minutes
Ball: number 4

Possible Formations

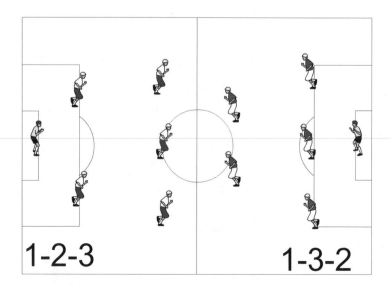

1-2-3   1-3-2

The Training Session

✓ The training session should involve fun and imaginative game like activities, as well as technical and tactical repetitive activities.

✓ Coaching technical skills is very important at this age as well as light tactical concepts.

✓ The training session has a technical and/or tactical theme (focus). For example: dribbling technique, or passing and receiving, or combination play.

✓ Small-sided directional games such as 3 v 3, 4v3, 4 v 4, 5v4 and 5v5 should be included as well. More detailed explanations regarding shape and positions.

✓ Training should always conclude with a 6v6 game with goalkeepers if possible (5 field players and 1 goalkeeper on each team).

✓ The duration of the training session should be 75-90 minutes.

Lesson Plan Design

The U10 training session should consist of about 6-8 activities. There should be a mixture of warm-up, dynamic, dynamic competitive and cool down activities. The design would be as follows:

1. Warm-up Activities
2. Stretch Activities
3. Dynamic Activity
4. Dynamic Activity
5. Dynamic Competitive Activity
6. Dynamic Competitive Activity
7. Dynamic Competitive Activity
8. Cool Down Activities

Sample Lesson Plan

1. Interactive Dribbling at an easy pace.
2. Stretch Activities
3. Gate Dribbling (with Gate Keepers)
4. Ball Tag
5. One versus One Challenge [1 v 1]
6. Four Corner Shooting
7. The Game 6v6
8. Controlled Juggling

Warm-Up Activities: The coach can use any of the *Dynamic Activities* as warm-up activities. The important thing to remember is that players perform in these activities at a *slower pace* and gradually increase their pace and output. These activities gradually warm-up the players' muscles and ligaments so that *proper stretching activities* can follow. The purpose of the warm-up is to allow the players to gradually build up to an intense training session, both physically and mentally.

Stretching Activities: There are two types of stretching that are appropriate for young players:

> Static Stretching – stationary stretching where muscle groups are slowly stretched for 20-30 seconds.

> Dynamic Stretching – explosive type stretching that replicates the body movement (actions) while playing the game. For example…swinging a leg front and back for 20-30 seconds.

Cool-Down Activities: These are Warm-up Activities, but are performed at the end of the training session. It's fun for the players to be challenged with these activities. For example…a juggling contest. The purpose of the cool-down is to allow the players to gradually come down from the intense training session, both physically and mentally.

U10 Training Activities Table

Dynamic	Dynamic Competitive
Interactive Dribbling	Ball Tag
Fast Footwork	Bandit Ball (Keep your ball)
Line-to-Line Dribbling	One versus One Challenge [1 v 1]
Dribble and Juggle	Two versus Two Challenge [2 v 2]
Gate Passing (2's, 3's or 4's)	Three versus Three Challenge [3 v 3]
Relay Challenge	Tag Team 1v2
Paint the field (2's, 3's or 4's)	Two versus One + One [2 v 1+1]
Passing by the Numbers	Passing by the Numbers with Bandit(s)
Circle Passing	Doctor-Doctor
Short-Short-Long Passing (Pattern Passing)	Timed Keep-Away (for points)
Serve-to-Self Receiving	Inside-Outside with Bandit(s)
Receiving Flighted Balls in Two's (2's)	Combat
Heading and Volleying in Two's (2's)	Shooting 2 v 1-2 v 1
Inside-Outside	Shooting with Uneven Numbers
Relay Shooting	Small-Sided Games with Neutral Players
Three-Touch Shooting (3-touch)	Small-Sided Games with Free Flank Players
	Corner Kick Challenge
	Four Corner Shooting
	The Game 6v6

**Use any of the U6 or U8 activities that you feel are appropriate and fun for the players.**

U10 Training Activities

Dynamic Activities

◆ **Interactive Dribbling**

Equipment:	One ball per player.
Set-up:	15 yard x 20 yard rectangular grid.
Activity:	All players dribble their soccer balls inside the rectangular grid moving through each other. They try to avoid collisions with other players and their soccer balls.
Variations:	On the coach's command (whistle) each player must roll the ball across their body to the left with the sole of their right foot or to the right with the sole of their left foot.
	On the coach's command (whistle) each player must push the ball forward with the soles of the feet, alternating left and right, 4 times, then continue dribbling.
	On the coach's command (whistle) each player must pull the ball backwards with the soles of the feet, alternating left and right, 4 times, then continue dribbling.

On the coach's command (whistle) the players dribble a little faster; on the next whistle the players dribble as fast as they can. Keep alternating between speeds by using the whistle or a specific command.

Coaching Considerations:

Fun, dribbling technique, use different surfaces of foot, keep ball close, keep head up, speed dribbling, simple decision making.

◆ Fast Footwork

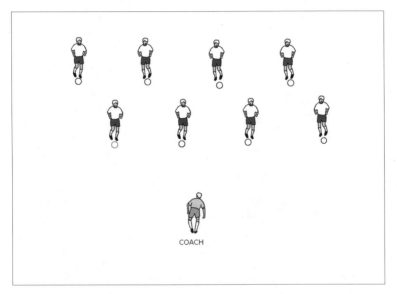

Equipment:	One ball per player
Set-up:	Players set up side-by-side in horizontal lines, behind the coach/leader 4-5 players to a line. Each player has a soccer ball.
Activity:	The coach or a player leads the group in choreographed footwork activities:

> Sole of foot ball taps (stationary).
> Inside of foot ball taps (stationary)
> Pull with sole and push with inside of same foot. Player must push the ball to his other foot and continue the same.
> Sole rolls forward and backward.
> Sole rolls side to side; left foot rolls to the right; right foot rolls to the left.

Add quarter turns every 10 seconds (right foot then left foot).
Add half turns every 10 seconds (right foot then left foot)

Coaching Considerations:

Repetitions; proper mechanics; quick, supple touches; head up.

◆ # Line-to-Line Dribbling

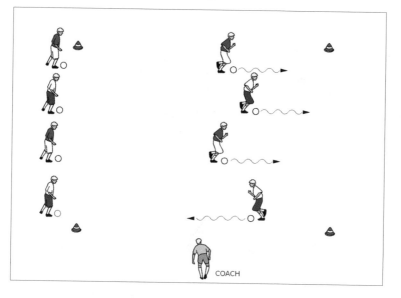

Equipment: One ball per player. Cones.

Set-up: Two lines made from cones approximately 20 yards apart. (adjust distance if necessary) Players pair up and form single file lines of two. Pairs line up side-by-side behind one of the cone lines.

Activity: On the coach's command, the first player in the pair dribbles to the opposite line and returns. When he returns, his partner dribbles to the other line and returns.

Variations: Dribble with the inside and outside of the right foot only on the way to the opposite line...dribble with the inside and outside of the left foot only on the way back to your partner.

Side rolls with the right foot only on the way to the opposite line...side rolls with the left foot only on the way back to your partner.

Coaching Considerations:

Repetitions; proper dribbling mechanics; quick, supple touches; head up.

♦ Dribble and Juggle

Equipment:	One ball per player.
Set-up:	Open area; no boundaries.
Activity:	All players dribble interactively. When the coach shouts, "Juggle!", the players must lift the ball up in the air with their feet and begin juggling for 5-10 seconds. After the juggling, the players resume dribbling.
Variations:	Same activity, but when the coach shouts, "Three!" (or any reasonable number) and the players must attempt to juggle 3 times.
	Same activity, but when the coach shouts, "Three!", 3 players join together and juggle one ball between the three of them for 15-20 seconds.

Repetitions; proper dribbling mechanics; quick, supple touches; head up while dribbling, eyes on ball while juggling.

♦ Gate Passing (2's, 3's or 4's)

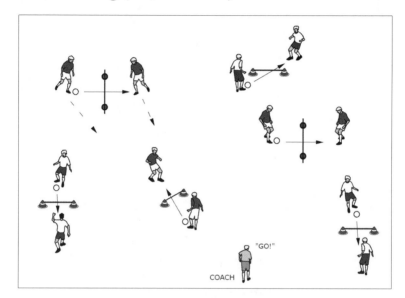

Equipment:	One ball for two players (pair). Cones.
Set-up:	Open area. Gates (2 cones about 1-2 yards apart) are placed at many different angles about 10 yards apart. Set up 1 gate per pair or 1 more gate than there are pairs (i.e. 5-6 gates for 5 pairs)
Activity:	Each pair passes their ball to each other freely through the gates. Once they pass their ball through one gate, they must find another gate to pass through.
Variations:	Same activity in groups of three or four. As you add more players to the group, position the gates farther apart.

Coaching Considerations:

Fun, passing and dribbling, changing direction, simple decision making (which gate to go through next), timing (when and how hard should I pass the ball to my partner), anticipation (can I pass my ball through that gate before someone else does?).

♦ Relay Challenge

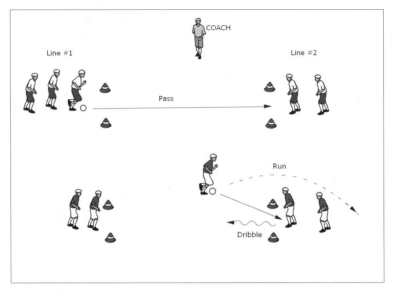

Equipment: Soccer balls and cones.

Set-up: Two players in single file line face one other player opposite them 10 yards away. The ball is placed with the first player in the line of two. Set up multiple lines so that all players are participating.

Activity: Pass-Receive-Dribble...First player in line #1 passes the ball to the player opposite him. After he passes the ball, he must run across and replace the player he passed to. The player receiving the ball must control it and dribble to line #1, giving the ball to the player located there. The sequence continues in this manner.

Variations: Two-Touch Passing...Similar to the sequence above. First player in line #1 passes the ball to the player opposite him. After he passes the ball, he must run across and replace the player he passed to. The player receiving the ball must control it on his first touch and pass it to line #1 on his second touch. Each time a pass is made the passer follows his pass to the opposite line.

Coaching Considerations:

Passing and receiving technique (keeping the ball close); proper preparation touch; passing accuracy and appropriate pace.

◆ Paint the Field (2's, 3's or 4's)

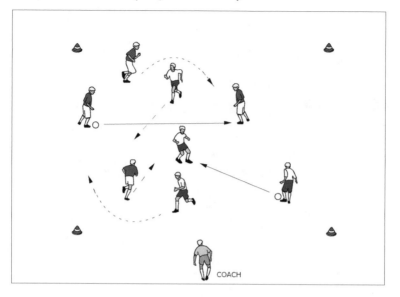

Equipment: Soccer balls. Pinnies (2 or 3 different colors).

Set-up: 20 yard x 30 yard rectangular grid. One ball per group of two, three or four. Color code the groups in different colored pinnies.

Activity: Players pass the ball within their group inside the grid. They pretend that their feet represent paint brushes and, as a group, they must paint the complete grid area as they pass and move.

Coaching consideration:

Intelligent movement, head up, preparing to receive the ball, surveying the area, looking for their target early, anticipation, passing accuracy and pace, keeping appropriate individual and group shape.

◆ Passing by the Numbers

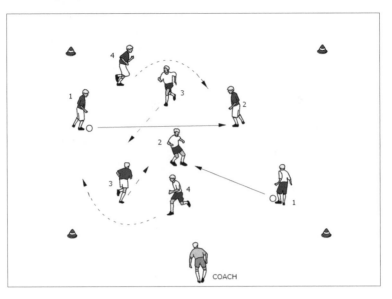

Equipment: Soccer balls. Pinnies (2 or 3 different colors).

Set-up: One ball per group of four or five players. The players in each group number themselves from one to four or from one to five.

Activity: Players pass the ball within their group by their consecutive numbers. One passes to two, then two passes to three, then three passes to four and four passes back to one. Players must be moving and the ball can never stop.

Coaching Considerations: Intelligent movement, head up, preparing to receive the ball, surveying the area, looking for their target early, anticipation, passing accuracy and pace, communication.

◆ Circle Passing

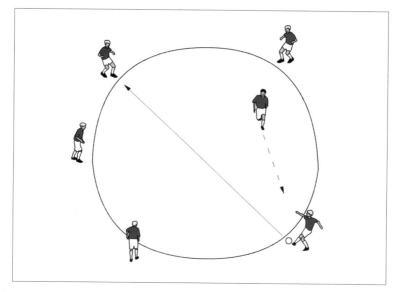

Equipment: 2-3 soccer balls.

Set-up: All the players position themselves around the center circle or a circle with a radius of 10-15 yards. One player has the soccer ball to begin the activity.

Activity: The player with the ball passes it to another player (it cannot be the players next to him), follows his pass and replaces the player he passed to. The player receiving the pass has two touches to control and pass the ball to someone else on the circle. He must also follow his pass and replace that player on the circle. This continues until the ball is played outside of the circle. Use Time as a challenge to the players…they must keep the ball moving, with the appropriate touches, inside the player circle for one minute!

Variations:

- Allow one touch only using one ball..
- Use 2 balls. Keep 2 balls moving for a timed period.

Coaching Considerations:

Intelligent movement, head up, preparing to receive the ball, surveying the area, looking for their target early, anticipation, passing accuracy and pace, communication.

95

◆ Short-Short-Long Passing (Pattern Passing)

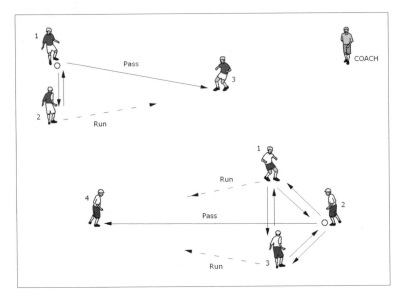

Equipment: Soccer balls. Pinnies (2 or 3 different colors).

Set-up: Open area. One ball per group of three.

Activity: Players pass the ball within their group. Two of the players position themselves about 5-10 yards apart and pass the ball back and forth to each other (short passes), while the third player (long player) drifts/checks about 20-25 yards away. After 4-5 short passes, the long player calls for the ball. The ball is played into the long player. The player that played the ball to the long player stays home, while the other player joins the long player. They begin to (short) pass to each other until the new "long" player calls for the ball. The activity continues in this manner for 2-3 minutes to develop a smooth rhythm in the passing sequence. Players consistently keep themselves and the ball moving. (Develop a triangle shape)

Variations: One ball per group of four. Similar to the activity described above, three players make short passes to each other, while one player drifts away. When the long ball is played, the passer stays home and the other two players join the "long" player. (Develop a "kite" type shape)

96

Intelligent movement, head up, preparing to receive the ball, surveying the area, looking for their target early, anticipation, passing accuracy and pace, keeping appropriate individual and group shape.

◆ Serve-to-Self Receiving

Equipment:	One ball per player.
Set-up:	25 yard x 30 yard rectangular grid.
Activity:	All players dribble their soccer balls inside the rectangular grid moving through each other. They try to avoid collisions with other players and their soccer balls. When the coach yells, "Laces", each player picks up their soccer ball and serves it in the air to themselves. They attempt to receive the ball with their "Laces" before it touches the ground. Once they have cushioned the ball to the ground, they continue to dribble around in the area. The coach can vary the command such as "Thigh" or "Chest" to promote other receiving surfaces.

Fun, receiving air balls with the laces, thighs and chest; getting to the ball in the air; comfort with the ball in the air; providing receiving surfaces for the ball; cushioning the ball; keeping the ball within dribbling distance.

◆ Receiving Flighted Balls in Two's (2's)

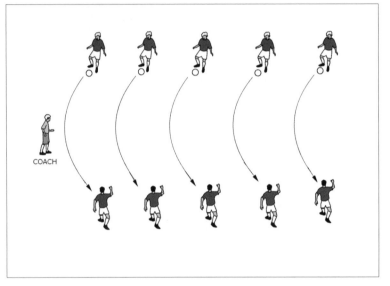

Equipment:	One soccer ball per two players.
Set-up:	Partners face each other approximately 5 yards apart. One of the players (the server) holds the ball in his hands.
Activity:	The server throws (serves) the ball (two-hand underhand) at different altitudes to the other player (the receiver). The receiver uses his chest, thigh or instep (laces) to receive the ball before it touches the ground. The receiver then passes the ball back to the server.
Variations:	The coach can determine which surfaces should be used to receive the ball. The coach can stipulate that two different surfaces must be used before the ball can hit the ground. The coach can increase the distance between the partners to provide more of a challenge.

The server can use appropriate throw-in technique or punt the ball to the receiver.

Coaching Considerations:

Proper receiving technique: good body balance, eyes on ball, body in-line with the path of the ball, movement to ball, appropriate touch on ball (cushion or propel).

♦ Heading and Volleying in Two's (2's)

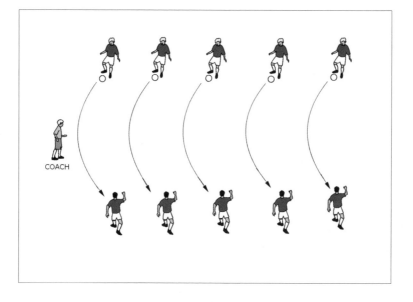

Equipment: One soccer ball per two players.

Set-up: Partners face each other approximately 5 yards apart. One of the players (the server) holds the ball in his hands.

Activity: The server throws (serves) the ball (two-hand underhand) at different altitudes to the other player (the receiver). The receiver heads or volleys the ball back to the server.

Variations:

- The coach can require that a receiving touch be made before the head or volley is made (two touch).

- The coach can increase the distance between the partners to provide more of a challenge.
- The server can use appropriate throw-in technique or punt the ball to the receiver.

Coaching Considerations:

Proper heading technique: good body balance, eyes on ball, body in-line with the path of the ball, movement to ball, tight neck, arched back (limbo), use upper forehead to strike ball.
Proper volleying technique: good body balance, eyes on ball, body in-line with the path of the ball, movement to ball, lock ankle, use inside of foot or instep to strike ball (pop!).

♦ Inside-Outside

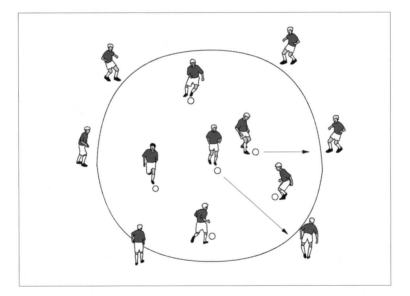

Equipment: One soccer ball per two players.

Set-up: Separate players into two groups. One group of players, without soccer balls, forms a circle with a diameter of about 30-35 yards. These players are the Windows. The other group of players, equipped with balls at their feet, position themselves inside the circle.

| *Activity:* | The players inside the circle (Insiders) dribble about the circle freely looking for an opportunity to pass the ball to a player on the perimeter of the circle (Outsiders). The Outsider one or two touch the ball back to the Insider. The Insider then controls the ball and looks for another Outsider to pass to. After approximately two minutes, the Insiders become Outsiders and vice versa. |

Variations:

- The Outsiders start with the ball in their hands. The Insiders move around freely inside the circle without a ball. The Insiders call for a ball from one of the Outsiders. The Outsider serves a ball (on the ground or in the air) to the Insider, who must one or two touch the ball back to the Outsider (server).

Coaching Considerations:

Intelligent movement, head up, preparing to receive the ball, surveying the area, looking for their target early, anticipation, passing accuracy and pace, keeping shape.

Proper receiving technique: good body balance, eyes on ball, body in-line with the path of the ball, movement to ball, appropriate touch on ball (cushion or propel).

Proper heading technique: good body balance, eyes on ball, body in-line with the path of the ball, movement to ball, tight neck, arched back (limbo), use upper forehead to strike ball.

Proper volleying technique: good body balance, eyes on ball, body in-line with the path of the ball, movement to ball, lock ankle, use inside of foot or instep to strike ball (pop!).

♦ Relay Shooting

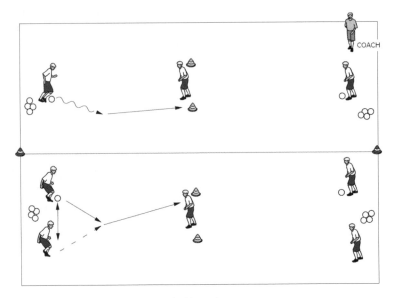

Equipment:	Soccer balls and cones.
Set-up:	Create goals, six yards wide, made from cones or flags, positioned side-by-side, horizontally across the field. Separate each goal by a distance of four yards. Three players are assigned to each goal. One player is positioned on one side of the goal approximately 15-20 yards away with a soccer ball (the first shooter); one player is in a similar position on the opposite side of the goal (second shooter); and one player is in the goal (the goalkeeper and third shooter). Place extra balls behind the shooters.
Activity:	The first shooter prepares the ball and shoots at the goal. The first shooter becomes the goalkeeper, the goalkeeper replaces the shooter and the second shooter prepares to shoot. The second shooter shoots the ball, follows his shot and becomes the goalkeeper. The goalkeeper replaces him. The third shooter prepares to shoot, etc. If the goalkeeper saves the ball, he turns and throws the ball to the opposite (next) shooter, before replacing the last shooter.
Variations:	Can assign five players to each group with 2 players on each side of the goal and one player in the goal. This allows a little more time for the players to get ready for their shot. The sequence is the same.

Proper technique: good body balance, appropriate preparation touch, good approach to the ball, appropriate kicking surface, eyes on ball, contact appropriate ball surface (under ball, center of ball, outside of ball, etc.), follow through, attack goal.

◆ Three-Touch Shooting (3-touch)

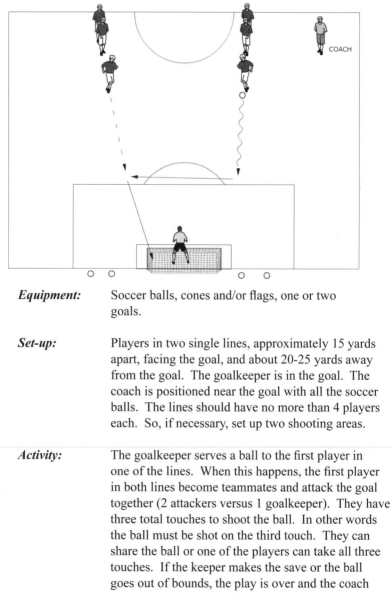

Equipment:	Soccer balls, cones and/or flags, one or two goals.
Set-up:	Players in two single lines, approximately 15 yards apart, facing the goal, and about 20-25 yards away from the goal. The goalkeeper is in the goal. The coach is positioned near the goal with all the soccer balls. The lines should have no more than 4 players each. So, if necessary, set up two shooting areas.
Activity:	The goalkeeper serves a ball to the first player in one of the lines. When this happens, the first player in both lines become teammates and attack the goal together (2 attackers versus 1 goalkeeper). They have three total touches to shoot the ball. In other words the ball must be shot on the third touch. They can share the ball or one of the players can take all three touches. If the keeper makes the save or the ball goes out of bounds, the play is over and the coach

serves to the next pair. If the keeper deflects the ball and it stays in play, the attackers are allowed 2 more touches to finish!

Variations:

- The coach can call out (manipulate) the number of total touches before the goalkeeper serves the ball.

Coaching Considerations:

Proper technique: good body balance, appropriate preparation touch, good approach to the ball, appropriate kicking surface, eyes on ball, contact appropriate ball surface (under ball, center of ball, outside of ball, etc.), follow through, attack goal. Proper decision making: to pass or not to pass, which foot or body surface to use when shooting, where to place the ball when shooting, follow-up to goal.

Dynamic Competitive Activities

♦ Ball Tag

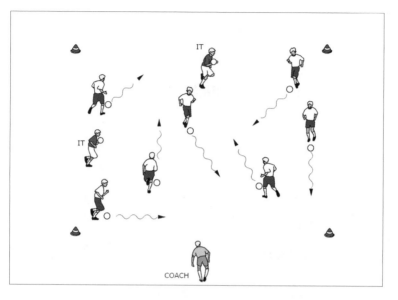

Equipment:	One soccer ball per player and cones.
Set-up:	15 yard x 20 yard grid (adjust for appropriate size). Two players are designated as **IT.** They must hold their ball in their hands. The rest of the players **(dribblers)** must begin with their ball at their feet.
Activity:	On the coach's command, the **ITs** must attempt to tag a **dribbler** with their ball (they cannot throw their ball at a **dribbler**). If they tag the dribbler, the dribbler becomes an **IT** (and must pick his ball up) and the **IT** becomes a **dribbler**. If any player leaves the grid or if their ball leaves the grid they immediately become an **IT** or remain an **IT.** When time is up each dribbler receives a point. Games should last a maximum of 2 minutes. Play multiple games so that all players have the opportunity to receive points.
Variations:	Set-up 2-4 safe houses within the grid (possibly in diagonal corners of the grid or all four corners of the grid). **Dribblers** can retreat to a safe house to avoid being tagged by an **IT**, but only one **dribbler** at a time can reside in a safe house. If another **dribbler**

decides to enter a safe house that is being occupied, the occupant must leave immediately to make room for the new resident.

Coaching Considerations:

Creative dribbling, decision making, scheming, FUN!

♦ Bandit Ball (Keep your ball)

Equipment:	One ball per player. Cones.
Set-up:	10 yard x 15 yard rectangular grid. 30-45 second games.
Activity:	All players are dribbling their soccer balls inside the grid, with the exception of one or two players, who do not have soccer balls (the bandits). When the coach says, "Watch out for bandits!", the bandits try to steal someone's ball. Once they have stolen a ball, they dribble it and try to keep possession of it; they are no longer a bandit. If a player loses a ball, he becomes a bandit and attempts to steal a ball. If a ball is kicked out of the grid, it cannot be brought back in. Start each game with new bandits. At the end of each game one point is awarded to the players who have possession of a ball.

Coaching Considerations:

Dribbling, individual possession (keeping the ball), shielding, constructive tackling (winning the ball), decision making, scheming.

♦ **One v One Challenge [1 v 1]**

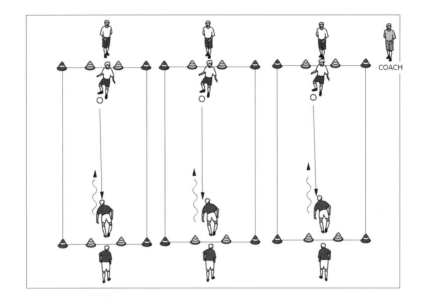

Equipment: Soccer balls, pinnies, cones, flags and/or small goals.

Set-up: Small rectangular fields, made with cones, approximately 15 yards long x 10 yards wide, located side-by-side. Place goals made from cones, flags or ready-made goals at each end of the field. Separate players into two color-coded (red and yellow) groups (teams). Send two players from each team to a field. The red pair gets at one end of the field and the yellow pair gets at the other end. One red player and one yellow player step onto the field ready to play against one another. The other player from each team rests behind the goal.

Activity: One of the players starts with the ball at his feet. On the coach's command, the player with the ball passes it to his opponent and the 1 v 1 competition begins. The players police themselves; in other words, they control the environment; they sort out rules, etc. All matches start at the same time and last for 30-45 seconds. After time is up, the two other players, who have rested, prepare to play the next match, while the two players, who have just played, rest.

Variations:

- Play with the goals inside the field so that there is space behind each goal to play (like ice hockey).
- When all players have played 2-3 games on a particular field, the coach can rotate a particular color pair to another field (i.e. all red pairs move to the next field).

Coaching Considerations:

Individual possession…dribbling, moves, change of pace and direction, shielding.
Individual penetration…when and how?
Individual defending…approach (speed, angle, distance)
Mentality…risky on the attack…restrained aggression on defense.

♦ Two versus Two Challenge [2 v 2]

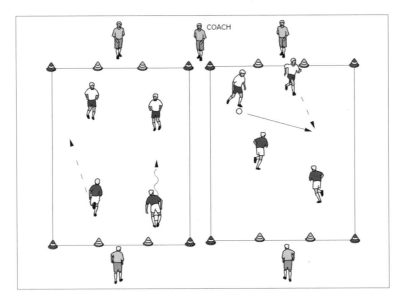

Equipment: Soccer balls, pinnies, cones, flags and/or small goals.

Set-up: Small rectangular fields, made with cones, approximately 20 yards long x 15 yards wide, located side-by-side. Place goals made from cones, flags or ready-made goals at each end of the field. Separate players into three color-coded (red, blue and yellow) groups (teams). Send two players from each team to a field. The red players defend one goal at one end of the field and the yellow players defend the other goal. The blue team rests while the red and yellow teams prepare to compete in a 2 v 2 game on the coach's command.

Activity: On the coach's command, the red and yellow teams play a 2 v 2 game. The players police themselves; in other words, they control the environment; they sort out rules, etc. All matches start at the same time and last for 1.5-2 minutes. After time is up, the blue team replaces the red team. The next 2 v 2 game begins, blue versus yellow, while the red team on each field rests. Finally, the red team plays the blue team, while the yellow team rests. (This is a round robin type of activity)

Variations:

- Play with the goals inside the field so that there is space behind each goal to play (like ice hockey).
- Play with goals located in diagonal corners of the field.
- When all three teams have played two games in the round robin format, the coach can rotate a particular color team to another field (i.e. all blue teams move to the next field).

Coaching Considerations:

Individual possession and possession in pairs (combination).
Individual and collective penetration…get in behind the opponents.
Pressure and cover on defense…defending in two's.
Mentality…risky on the attack…restrained aggression on defense.

◆ Three versus Three Challenge [3 v 3]

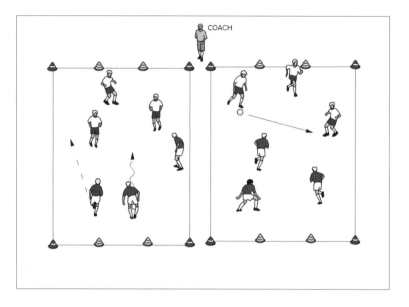

Equipment:	Soccer balls, pinnies, cones, flags and/or small goals.
Set-up:	Small rectangular fields, made with cones, approximately 25 yards long x 20 yards wide, located side-by-side. Place goals made from cones, flags or ready-made goals at each end of the field. Separate players into two color-coded (red and blue) groups (teams). Send three players from each team to a field. The red players defend one goal at one end of the field and the blue players defend the other goal.
Activity:	On the coach's command, the red and blue teams play a 3 v 3 game. The players police themselves; in other words, they control the environment; they sort out rules, etc. All matches start at the same time and last for 3-4 minutes. Play 4-5 matches.
Variations:	
	Make the goals larger and play with goalkeepers. Play with the goals inside the field so that there is space behind each goal to play (like ice hockey). Play with goals located in diagonal corners of the field. Play with no goals, but instead have the extra players work as targets for two competing teams. The target can move freely along the horizontal end line.

Coaching Considerations:

Individual possession and possession in pairs (combination).

Individual and collective penetration; get in behind the opponents.

Pressure and cover on defense; defending in two's.

Mentality; risky on the attack; restrained aggression on defense.

♦ Tag Team 1v2

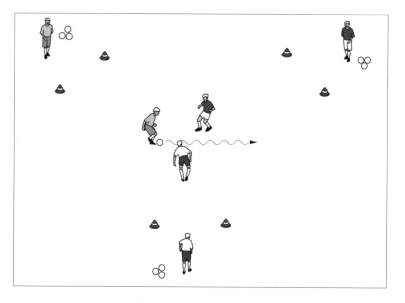

Equipment:	Soccer balls, pinnies and cones.
Set-up:	Three gates (made from cones about 2 steps wide) set up about 15-20 yards apart in a triangular fashion. Three pairs of players, each pair in different color pinnies, positioned at one of the gates. One player from each pair steps in front of his gate prepared to play. One of the three players will be given the ball by the coach. The other player in the pair will rest until his teammate tags him.
Activity:	On the coach's command play begins. Each of the three players defends one gate, but can score on the two other gates (i.e. red can score on the yellow or blue gates). One player has the ball while the other

two players try to steal it. A point is awarded when a player dribbles through one of the opponent's gates from inside the triangular area. Play is allowed outside the triangular area, but no points are awarded if a player dribbles through the back of the gate from outside the triangle. At any time during the competition, a player can tag their partner, who then replaces him in the competition. Teammates add their points together at the end of the competition. Each competition should last no longer than three minutes.

Coaching Considerations:

Individual possession (dribbling and shielding), aggressiveness, tough mentality, defending, (constructive tackling).

♦ **Two versus One + One [2 v 1+1]**

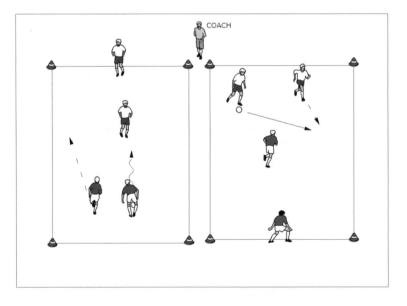

Equipment: Soccer balls, pinnies and cones.

Set-up: Small rectangular fields, made with cones, approximately 20 yards long x 15 yards wide, located side-by-side. Separate players into two color-coded (red and yellow) groups (teams). Send two players from each team to a field. The red pair gets at one end of the field and the yellow pair gets at the other end. Two red players and one yellow player step onto the field ready to play. The other yellow player is positioned on his end-line.

Activity: On the coach's command, the two red players start with the ball and attack the yellow team's end-line. The yellow field player and the yellow end-line player defend their end-line. The yellow end-line player cannot move off of the end-line, but may move horizontally along the line to prevent the red team from scoring. To score a point, the team in possession of the ball must dribble or pass the ball to their teammate over the end-line. When the red team has possession of the ball it becomes two red players versus one yellow field player and one yellow end-line player. Thus, 2 v 1+1. When a point is scored for the red team or yellow wins possession of the ball, yellow plays with two field players and red must drop one of their players back to defend (position themselves on) their end-line. The game continues in this manner until one team scores five points or until the players have played for 5 minutes.

Coaching Considerations:

Individual possession and possession in pairs (combination). Individual and collective penetration…get in behind the opponents.
Intelligent pressure, fall back and delay on defense… defending in two's.
Mentality…risky on the attack…restrained aggression on defense.

♦ Passing by the Numbers with Bandit(s)

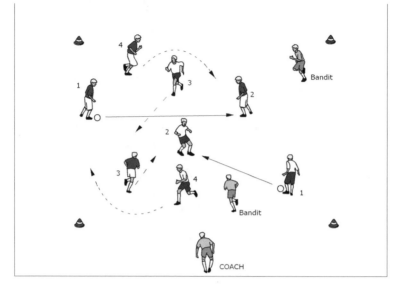

Equipment: Soccer balls, cones and pinnies (3 different colors).

Set-up: 15 yard x 20 yard rectangular grids. Each group is color-coded, one group in yellow and one group in red. One ball per group of four or five players. One group per grid. The players in each group number themselves from one to four or from one to five. Select one bandit per grid who will wear blue.

Activity: Players pass the ball within their group by their consecutive numbers. One passes to two, then two passes to three, then three passes to four and four passes back to one. Players must be moving and the ball can never stop. Everyone in the group receives a point if the ball is passed successfully through the cycle. Once through the cycle play continues to see how many cycles the team can get through.
The bandit assigned to a particular grid must try to win possession of the ball and dribble it out of the grid. If successful he gets a point and can replace the person that he stole the ball from.

114

Intelligent movement, head up, preparing to receive the ball, positioning away from and in support of the ball, surveying the area, looking for their target early, anticipation, passing accuracy and pace, communication.

♦ Doctor-Doctor

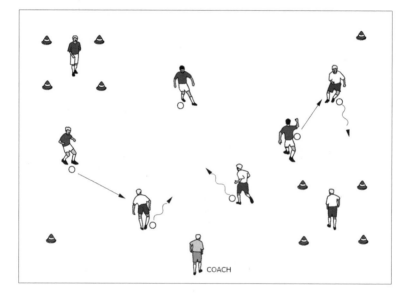

Equipment:	Soccer balls, cones and pinnies.
Set-up:	Rectangular field 25 yards x 20 yards. Two smaller grids, 5 yards x 5 yards, inside the larger field, located at diagonal (opposite) corners. Separate players into two color-coded (red and yellow) groups (teams). Select one player, without a ball, from each team who will be called the Doctor and will reside in his hospital (one of the corner grids). All other players are equipped with a soccer ball.
Activity:	On the coach's command the game begins. Players from both teams dribble their soccer balls and attempt to hit an opposing player with their soccer ball by passing the ball at him below the knees. If a player gets hit by the opponent, he must stop, pick his ball up, hold it on top of his head and yell ,"Doctor!

115

Doctor!". Their Doctor can free them by running out of his hospital and tagging the player who has been injured. When the Doctor is in his hospital, no one can hit him. But the Doctor must be careful not to get hit by the opponent when he leaves the hospital or the game will be over very fast because there will be no one to free the Doctor! The game is over when all the players and the Doctor of one of the teams are injured. After each game, change the Doctors.

Variation: The way to hit a player is to pass your ball so that it hits their ball (like marbles), instead of hitting the player.

Coaching Considerations:

Creative dribbling, passing accuracy, timing of passes, scheming, agility, balance, FUN!

◆ Timed Keep-Away (for points)

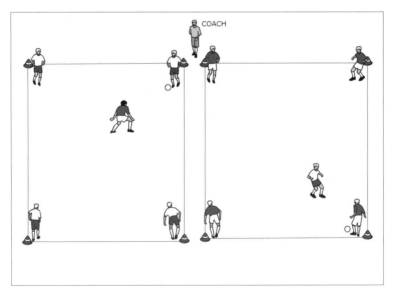

Equipment: Soccer balls, cones and pinnies (2 different colors).

Set-up: 15 yard x 15 yard rectangular grids. Adjust size of grid for larger numbers. Separate players into two color-coded (red and yellow) groups (teams). Put four yellow players (attackers) and one red player (defender) in one grid (4 v 1). Put four red players (attackers) and one yellow player (defender) in the other grid (4 v 1).

Activity: On the command, "Play!" the four attackers attempt to keep the ball away from the one defender in each grid. The attackers score one point by connecting three consecutive passes without losing possession to the defender. The defender scores a point if he can win possession of the ball and dribble it out of the grid. If the defender simply interrupts the possession by the attackers or if he kicks the ball out of the grid, no point is awarded. If the ball leaves the grid and goes out of play, an attacker re-starts the game immediately by retrieving a ball from outside the grid. If the attackers only connect two passes before the defender destroys it, the passing sequence starts again. Points are accumulative and play is continuous for 1 minute. At the conclusion of each 1 minute competition, the teams (red attackers and defender; yellow attackers and defender) get together and add up their points. The next game begins with a new defender in each grid. Make sure that you play at least five games so that each player works as a defender. The team with the most points at the end of the series of competitions wins!

Variations: Player with different numbers: 3 v 1, 4 v 2, 5 v 2, etc.

Coaching Considerations:

Passing and receiving, technical and tactical speed, play under the pressures of time, space and opponent(s), anticipation, individual and group shape.

◆ Inside-Outside with Bandit(s)

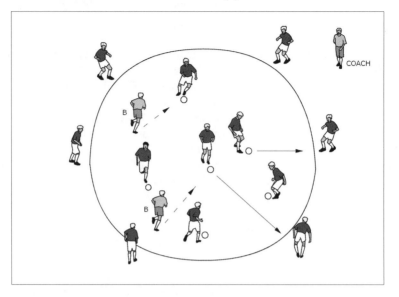

Equipment: One soccer ball per two players.

Set-up: Separate players into two groups. One group of players, without soccer balls, forms a circle with a diameter of about 30-35 yards. These players are the Outsiders. The other group of players, equipped with balls at their feet, position themselves inside the circle (Insiders). Select one or two players to act as bandits (in different color pinnies).

Activity: The Insiders dribble about the circle looking for an opportunity to pass the ball to an Outsider. The Outsider can one or two touch the ball back to the Insider. The Insider then controls the ball and looks for another Outsider to pass to. The bandits try to disrupt the flow of play and/or steal a ball. If they are successful they are no longer a bandit, but are replaced by the person whose ball they stole. After approximately two minutes, the Insiders become Outsiders and vice versa.

Coaching Considerations:

Intelligent movement, head up, preparing to receive the ball, surveying the area, looking for their target early, anticipation, passing accuracy and pace, keeping shape, under pressure.

Proper receiving technique: good body balance, eyes on ball, body in-line with the path of the ball, movement to ball, appropriate touch on ball (cushion or propel), under pressure.

Proper heading technique: good body balance, eyes on ball, body in-line with the path of the ball, movement to ball, tight neck, arched back (limbo), use upper forehead to strike ball, under pressure.

Proper volleying technique: good body balance, eyes on ball, body in-line with the path of the ball, movement to ball, lock ankle, use inside of foot or instep to strike ball (pop!), under pressure.

♦ Combat

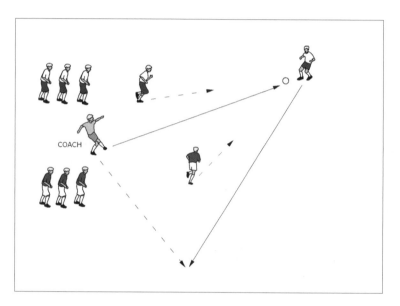

Equipment: One ball. Scrimmage vests in two colors.

Set-up: Open area; no boundaries. Coach equipped with the soccer ball. Color-coded players lined up in two single file lines; one line on the right side of the coach and one line on the left side of the coach facing toward the open area.

Activity: When the coach kicks the ball out into the open area, the activity begins. If, before the coach kicks the ball out, he shouts, "Yellow!", then two players from the yellow group and one player from the red group chase the ball and we have a 2 v 1 competition in favor of the yellow team. A point is awarded to the team that gets the ball back to the coach within

119

a specified amount of time. When the coach gets the ball back, he kicks it out again for the next set of players.

After the coach kicks out the ball, he should move away from the other players. There are two reasons for this. One, risk to the other players. Two, the players in the competition will look back for their target, anticipating how to turn on their opponent..

Variations: The coach can manipulate the activity by making the competition 3 v 2 or 4 v 3 simply by shouting a color before he kicks the ball out.

Coaching Considerations:

Attacking and defending skills and decision making with uneven numbers, shielding, dribbling to beat an opponent, tackling, looking for a target (the coach), passing pace and accuracy, combination play, basic shapes.

♦ **Shooting 2 v 1-2 v 1**

Equipment: Soccer balls, cones and pinnies.

Set-up: Make a long grid (corridor #1) 5 yards wide x 24 yards long, separated into three consecutive grids, each 5 yards wide x 8 yards with a goal (6ft high x 18 ft long) at one end of corridor #1. Set-up an identical grid (corridor #2) next to the first one going in the opposite direction with the goal at the opposite end. Position all players, except for six, into two single file lines at the end of one of the corridors. The other six players are wearing pinnies and will be positioned as follows:

- ✓ One on the back line of the 1st grid in corridor #1 (front defender #1).
- ✓ One on the back line of the 2nd grid in corridor #1 (back defender #1).
- ✓ One in the goal in corridor #1 (goalkeeper #1).
- ✓ One on the back line of the 1st grid in corridor #2 (front defender #2).
- ✓ One on the back line of the 2nd grid in corridor #2 (back defender #2).
- ✓ One in the goal in corridor #2 (goalkeeper #2).

The defenders can only defend on their assigned line!

Activity: On the coach's command, the first player in each single file line play as a pair and attack the two defenders and the goalkeeper in corridor #1. They must stay within the corridor. If they make it past the two defenders, they attempt a shot on goal. Whether they are successful or not, they proceed to corridor #2 and begin the activity again. When this happens the next pair of players begin the activity in corridor #1. It is a rotational, continuous activity. Be sure to change the defenders and goalkeepers often.

Coaching Considerations:

Simple combination play, attacking mentality, finishing.

♦ Shooting with Uneven Numbers

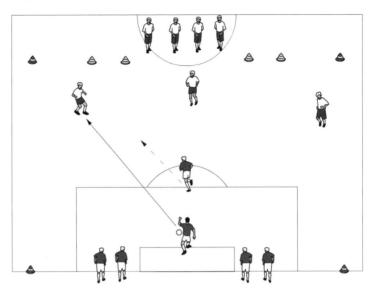

Equipment: Soccer balls, cones, flags, goals and pinnies.

Set-up: Rectangular grid 30 yards wide x 25 yards long (wider than long). A goal centered at one end of the field and two counter attack goals (made from flags or cones) positioned just inside the corners at the opposite end of the field. Separate your players into two groups. Put one third of the players in yellow pinnies (defenders and goalkeepers); put the remaining players in red pinnies (attackers). Select three attackers and two defenders to compete. The three attackers space themselves out at the end of the field opposite from the goal. The defenders take up positions at the other end of the field. One of the defenders acts as a goalkeeper, but must play with his feet whenever possible (3 v 2). The coach can set up two of these field spaces, if necessary, to get more player involvement.

Activity: The goalkeeper starts the competition by kicking the ball (punt or from the ground) in the direction of the attackers. The 3 v 2 begins. The three attackers attempt to score on the goal (1 point awarded). The two defenders attempt to win possession of the ball and kick it through one of the counter-attack goals (2 points awarded). Competitions should last a maximum of 2 minutes. Rotate players in appropriately.

Variations: Play with different numbers (4v3, 5v4, etc.) Adjust the field space to suit the number of players.

Coaching Considerations:

Technical speed (dribbling, receiving, passing, heading, shooting, tackling) under pressure, tactical speed under pressure (when, where, how, why?), playing with numbers up, playing with numbers down.

◆ Small-Sided Games with Neutral Players

Equipment: Soccer balls, pinnies, cones, flags and/or small goals.

Set-up: Small rectangular field, made with cones, approximately 30 yards long x 40 yards wide, located side-by-side. Place goals made from cones, flags or ready-made goals at each end of the field. Separate players into two color-coded (red and yellow) groups (teams). Select two players who will wear blue pinnies (neutral players). Send four players from each team to a field. The red players defend one goal at one end of the field and the yellow players defend the other goal. The two blue players join the field as neutral players. The blue players only play with the team in possession of the ball, giving them a numerical advantage [i.e. 4 v 4+2 means: six attacking players versus four defending players].

Activity: On the coach's command, the red and yellow teams, along with the blue neutral players, play a 4 v 4+2 game. The players police themselves; in other words, they control the environment; they sort out rules, etc. All matches start at the same time and last for 3-4 minutes. Play enough games so that all players rotate in as the neutral player.

Variations:

Play 5 v 5+1 games. (Adjust fields appropriately)

Coaching Considerations:

Individual possession and possession in pairs (combination). Individual and collective penetration...get in behind the opponents.
Pressure and cover on defense...defending in two's, three's and four's.
Using the extra neutral player to your advantage.
Mentality...risky on the attack...restrained aggression on defense.

♦ Small-Sided Games with Free Flank Players

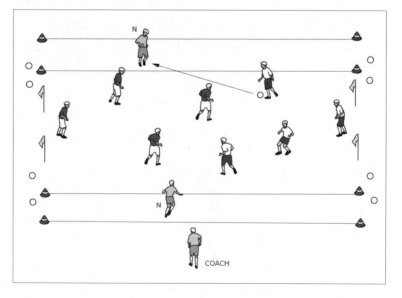

Equipment: Soccer balls, cones, flags, goals and pinnies.

Set-up: Rectangular field(s), 30 yards x 40 yards (adjust field size if necessary). Goals centered at each end of the field. Separate players into two color-coded (red and yellow) teams. Select one player from each team to be flank players and outfit them in a blue pinnie. Organize a 4 v 4 or 5 v 5 on the field of play (these numbers include the goalkeeper). Position the flank players, one on each side of the field, outside the touch lines. The flank players can move freely up and down the touch line, but cannot enter the field of play.

Activity: This is a typical 4 v 4 or 5 v 5 game, except that the flank players are totally free outside the field of play (no one from either team can pressure them). Either team can pass to a flank player. Once a flank player receives the ball from a team, he must play for that team and only has a maximum of 3 touches to return the ball into play to his team.

Variations: Set up special outside lanes for the free flank players. Position one red player and one yellow player on each flank to offer pressure to each other. Allow free switching of players from inside the field to the flanks, but only one player from each team is allowed in the flank at any given time.

Coaching Considerations:

Proper use of flank players (getting ball wide immediately), overlapping runs, crosses, shots with the head, volley and half-volley shots, defending crossed balls, playing under pressure.

◆ Corner Kick Challenge

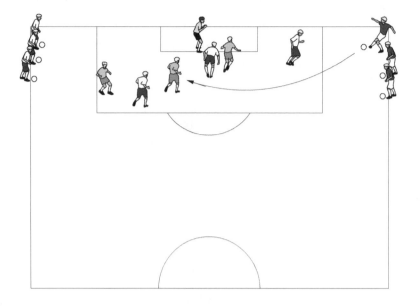

Equipment:	Soccer balls, cones, flags, goals and pinnies.
Set-up:	One end of a regulation U10 field with corners marked off and a goal centered on the end-line. Organize four teams of three or four players each. Color-code the teams so that each team is in a different color. The red team positions themselves at one corner of the field with soccer balls, the yellow team positions themselves at the other corner of the field with their balls, the blue and green teams position themselves in the penalty area or an area slightly larger than the penalty area in front of the goal. Position a goalkeeper in the goal.
Activity:	The red and yellow teams alternate taking corner kicks. The blue and green teams compete against each other trying to score from the corner kick. The play stays live until a goal is scored, the ball goes out of play/area or time is up. When a goal is scored from a corner kick, the corner kicker is awarded a point, as well as the player who scored the goal. After a determined number of corner kicks are taken, the red and yellow teams switch positions with the blue and green teams and a new competition begins. The players can play multiple rounds of this activity. At the end of the competition, each team should get together and total the points of each player on their

team creating a team score. Therefore it is imperative that each player keep their own score throughout the competition.

Variations: One of the teams in the penalty area defends the corner kicks, while the other team tries to score. A defender gets a point if he successfully clears the ball out of the penalty area.

Coaching Considerations:

Corner Kick technique and repetition, timing of receiving and striking corner kicks, defending corner kicks, competitive spirit, fun!

◆ Four Corner Shooting

Equipment: Enough balls for all players, pinnies, goals, cones and flags if available.

Set-up: 30 yard x 25 yard rectangular grid (field). Goals at each end of the field. Coach positioned outside the field at the mid-line with all of the balls. Two teams of players, in different colored pinnies; half of each team lined up in single file behind a specified corner cone (4 lines); one team at one end and one team at the other end. Goals are designated for each team and goalkeepers are positioned in each goal.

Activity: When the coach serves a ball into the field of play, the first 2 players in each of the 4 lines enters the field and a 5 v 5 competition begins (4 field players and a goalkeeper for each team). Play continues until a goal is scored or the ball goes out of bounds. When this happens, the players must get off the field quickly and get back in their line. When they are off the field, the coach sends another ball into the field, and the competition continues with the next players in each line.

Coaching Considerations:

Technique under the pressure of a game, decision making in the competitive game environment, triangular and rectangular shapes, passing and receiving, shooting, FUN!

◆ The Game 6v6

Equipment: Enough balls for all players, cones and flags if available.

Set-up: 40 yard x 50 yard rectangular grid (field). Goals at each end made out of cones or flags, approximately 5-6 steps wide. Balls are placed outside and behind the goals. 6 v 6 on the field.

Activity: Start play with a kick-off from the center of the field. Use US Youth Soccer modified rules.

128

The U12 Age Group

The effect of the role model is very important at this stage of development. Hero worship, identification with successful teams/ players and a hunger for imaginative skills typify the mentality of this age. Players at this age can be extremely self-critical. This is the "Golden Age of Learning" and the most important age for skill development. Demonstration is very important and the players learn best by doing. This is an appropriate time to emphasize and teach the ***Principles*** of play:

Attacking Principles	*Defensive Principles*
Penetration	*Recovery (Immediate Chase)*
Support	*Pressure*
Mobility	*Cover*
Width	*Balance*
Depth (length)	*Compactness*
Improvisation (deception, creativity)	*Counter Attack*

For more information on attacking and defensive principles please refer to Tactics page 173-177.

Role of Coach

The role of the coach in the U12 age group is to be a patient and motivating teacher. At this level, in addition to understanding technique, coaches should be able to provide environments conducive to problem solving (decision-making) by the players utilizing guided discovery methods. Specifically, individual and small group tactics should be the focus of the training sessions.

License Requirement

The U10/U12 State Youth Module is required. The State E License and the National Youth License are recommended.

The U12 Player Characteristics

Mental/Psychological (cognitive)

Fertile period for learning…eager to learn
Ability to sequence thought and actions and perform more
complex tasks…can simultaneously run, strike a ball and think!
Ability to use more abstract thought to meet the demands of
the game (i.e. well-timed overlapping run)
Use their teammates to solve game problems
Training must replicate the game

Physical (psychomotor)

Continue to gain a tremendous amount of physical strength,
endurance and power
Flexibility training is key to prevention of injury
More confident with physical technical demands above
their waist (receiving with the chest; heading the ball)
Goalkeeping skills are becoming refined
Children continue to be in growth spurts
Overuse injuries occur when age appropriate development
is ignored
Height can be well over 5 feet and weight can be 100+ lbs
The age range for the beginning of pubescence in girls is
7-14, with the average being 10 years of age
The age range for the beginning of pubescence in boys is
9-16, with the average being 12 years of age

Socially (psychosocial)

Gender differences are more apparent
Whether a child enters puberty early or late has important
psychological implications regarding relationships with
their teammates
Spend more time with their friends and less time with their
parents
Children tend to conform to peer pressure
Developing a conscience, morality and a scale of values

What to Teach U12 Players (Game Components)

Technique (skills):

Dribbling
To beat an opponent (penetration)
To possess (shielding)

Feints with the Ball
Subtle body movements to unbalance the opponent

Receiving Air Balls with Feet, Thighs and Chest
Away from pressure
To beat an opponent

Heading to Score Goals and for Clearances
Accuracy (direction)

Timing

Finishing
Chipping
Bending
Toe

Introduce Half Volley and Volley Shooting

Passing
Deceptive use of foot surface (toe, outside of foot, heel)

Crossing to Near Post and Penalty Spot Space
Driven

Flighted

Introduce Slide Tackle
Timing
Poke Tackle

Goalkeeping (skills)

Footwork for Goalkeepers
Post to post (lateral)
Forward

Throwing
Side-arm

Round-house

Baseball

Kicking

Drop-kick

Diving

Step and Collapse (low)

Step and slide onto forearms and thighs

Angle Play

Fast footwork

Body shape

Introduce Parrying and Boxing

One hand

Two hands

Psychology (mental and social):

- Teamwork
- Confidence
- Desire
- Mental rehearsal
- Intrinsic motivation
- Handling distress
- How to learn from each match
- Sportsmanship
- Parental involvement
- Emotional management

Fitness (conditioning):

- Speed
- Strength
- Aerobic exercise
- Proper warm-up and cool-down now mandatory

Tactics (decisions):

- 2 v 1 through 3 v 3 attacking & defending
- Introduce the principles of play
- Verbal & visual communication for all players
- Half-time analysis
- Beginning to identify potential roles for players

(goalkeeper, defender, midfielder &/or forward)
- Commanding the goalmouth by the goalkeeper
- Near post play by the goalkeeper
- Saving penalty kicks
- Simple set play patterns
- Speed in setting up walls

Rules:

Offsides

US Youth Soccer Modifications to The Game

Playing numbers:	8v8 (with goalkeepers)
Field Dimensions:	
Length	70-80 yards
Width	45-55 yards
Goal Dimensions:	
Height	6 feet
Width	18 feet
Duration:	two periods of 30 minutes
Ball:	number 4

Possible Formations

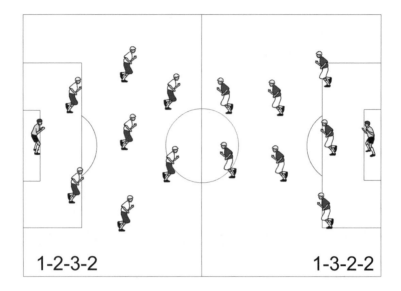

1-2-3-2   1-3-2-2

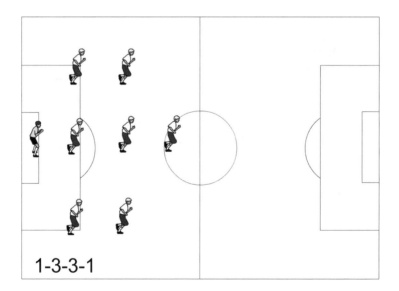

1-3-3-1

The Training Session

✓ The training session should involve fun and imaginative game like activities, as well as technical and tactical repetitive activities.
✓ The training session has a technical and/or tactical theme (focus). For example: dribbling technique and/or 1 v 1 decision making.
✓ Introduction to functional training (position specific) is appropriate.
✓ Small-sided directional games such as: 4 v 4, 5v4,5v5, 6v5, 6v6 and 7v6 should be included as well.
✓ Training should always conclude with a 8v8 game with goalkeepers if possible. (7 field players and 1 goalkeeper on each team) The duration of the training session should be 90 minutes.

Lesson Plan Design

The U12 training session should consist of about 6-8 activities. There should be a mixture of warm-up, dynamic, dynamic competitive and cool down activities. The design would be as follows:

1. Warm-up Activities
2. Stretching Activities
3. Dynamic Activity
4. Dynamic Stretching Activity
5. Dynamic Competitive Activity
6. Dynamic Competitive Activity
7. Dynamic Competitive Activity
8. Cool Down Activities

Sample Lesson Plan

1. Inter-Passing in Groups
2. Stretching
3. Passing by the Numbers
4. Dynamic Stretching

5. Inside-Outside with Bandits
6. Small Sided Games with Neutral Players (4 v 4+1 to end-zones)
7. The Game 8v8
8. One-Two or Two-One Juggling

Warm-Up Activities: The coach can use any of the *Dynamic Activities* as warm-up activities. The important thing to remember is that players perform in these activities at a *slower pace* and gradually increase their pace and output. These activities gradually warm-up the players' muscles and ligaments so that *proper stretching activities* can follow. The purpose of the warm-up is to allow the players to gradually build up to an intense training session, both physically and mentally.

Stretching Activities: There are two types of stretching that are appropriate for young players:

> Static Stretching – stationary stretching where muscle groups are slowly stretched for 20-30 seconds.
>
> Dynamic Stretching – explosive type stretching that replicates the body movement (actions) while playing the game. For example…swinging a leg front and back for 20-30 seconds.

Cool-Down Activities: These are Warm-up Activities, but are performed at the end of the training session. It's fun for the players to be challenged with these activities. For example…a juggling contest. The purpose of the cool-down is to allow the players to gradually come down from the intense training session, both physically and mentally.

U12 Training Activities Table

Dynamic	Dynamic Competitive
Interactive Dribbling with Take-Overs	Grid Combat with Bandits
Box to Box Dribbling Competition	Timed Four versus Two Keep-Away (4v2)
One-Two or Two-One Juggling	Timed Five versus Two Keep-Away (5v2)
Middle Man…Passing and Receiving Low Balls	Small-Sided Games with Neutral Players
Middle Man…Serving and Receiving Air Balls	Small-Sided Games with Free Flank Players
Short-Short-Long Passing (Pattern Passing)	Zone 1v2+1v2 Competition
Circle Passing (Two Balls)	Zone 1v3+1v3 Competition
Passing by the Numbers (Two Balls)	Zone 2v3+2v3 Competition
Inter-Passing in Groups (Shape)	Zone 2v4+2v4 Competition
Middle Zone Shooting (Sequence Shooting)	Shooting with Uneven Numbers
	Four Corner Shooting
	The Game 8v8

All of the U10 activities are appropriate and fun for the U12 players. Our coaching considerations become a little more tactical in nature and our expectations are higher.

U12 Training Activities

Dynamic Activities

♦ Interactive Dribbling with Take-Overs.

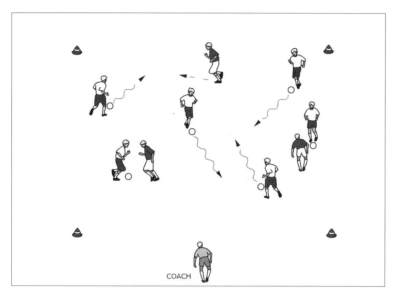

Equipment: One ball per player.

Set-up: 15 yd x 20 yd rectangular grid. All players have a
ball at their feet (ball carriers) except for 3-4 players,
who do not have a ball (free players).

Activity: The ball carriers dribble their soccer balls inside the
rectangular grid moving through each other. They try
to avoid collisions with other players and their soccer
balls. Whenever the opportunity presents itself, a ball
carrier, will give their ball to one of the free players
by using a take-over (like a hand-off in football but
done with the feet).

Coaching Considerations:

Fun, dribbling technique, keep head up, simple
decision making, communication, judgment (take-
overs are performed right foot to right foot or left foot
to left foot).

◆ Box to Box Dribbling Competition

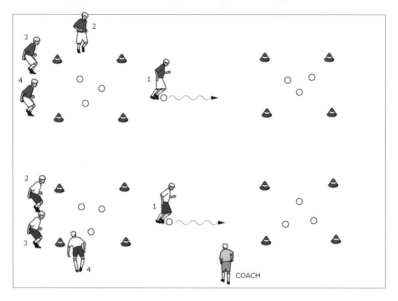

Equipment: One ball per player.

Set-up: Set up corridors, side-by-side consisting of two 3 yard x 3 yard grids approximately 15-20 yards apart. Four players assigned to each corridor. The four players form a team. Four balls are placed in one of the two grids at the same end of each corridor. Players are positioned next to the grid with the balls. Players number themselves from 1 to 4.

Activity: On the coach's command, player #1 from each team dribbles one of the balls from the grid to the opposite grid, leaves the ball and returns home. Once player #1 is home, player #2 dribbles a ball from the grid to the opposite grid and leaves it there, returning home without the ball. This continues until player #4 returns home without a ball. When player #4 returns home, player #1 sprints to the opposite grid, takes a ball and dribbles it home. This activity continues until player #4 is home with a ball and all four balls are in the original grid. The balls must be inside the grid for the team to win the competition.

Coaching Considerations:

Speed dribbling…running with the ball, controlling the ball with the feet, quick change of direction, competition.

♦ One-Two or Two-One Juggling

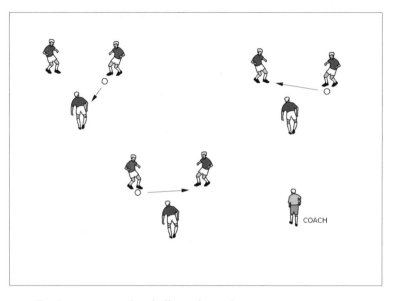

Equipment:	One ball per three players.
Set-up:	Players form a triangle, with each player approximately 5 yards from the other two players. One of the players is the server and holds the ball in his hands. The other players are the jugglers.
Activity:	The server will serve an air ball approximately 5-10 feet in the air to one of the two jugglers. Before the ball is served, the server must say, "One-Two!" or "Two-One!" If the server says, "One-Two!", the receiver must play the ball in the air with his first touch to the other juggler, who must juggle it with his first touch and return it in the air to the server's hands, with his second touch. Thus…One (touch)-Two (touches). If he says, "Two-One!", the receiver must juggle the ball with the first touch and deliver it in the air with the second touch to the other juggler, who must return it in the air with one touch to the server's hands. Thus…Two (touches)-One (touch).
Variations:	Play this juggling game while moving. Set up many 3-player teams and have a competition to see which team can go through the most consecutive sequences without dropping the ball to the ground.

Coaching Considerations:

Anticipation, preparation touches, placement of the ball, touch.

♦ Middle Man...Passing and Receiving Low Balls

COACH

Equipment: Soccer balls, cones.

Set-up: Three players in single file, approximately 10-15 yards apart. Two outside players and one inside or middle player. The two outside players have a ball at their feet.

Activity: On the coach's command, the outside players alternate passing their ball to the middle player. The middle player receives the ball and plays it back to the passer.

Variations:

- The middle player plays it back with one touch or two touches.
- The middle player:

  ✓ receives the ball with the inside of the foot, then plays it back to the passer.
  ✓ receives the ball with the outside

142

of the foot, then plays it back to the passer.

✓ prepares the ball close to the his body before playing it back to the passer.

✓ prepares the ball away from his body before playing it back to the passer.

• Only one ball is used. On the coach's command, one of the outside players passes the ball to the middle player, who must turn with the ball on the first touch and pass it to the opposite outside player.

Coaching Considerations: Passing and receiving technique, proper 1st touch (preparation touch), receiving with inside and outside of the foot, passing accuracy and pace, passing with inside and outside of the foot.

♦ Middle Man...Serving and Receiving Air Balls

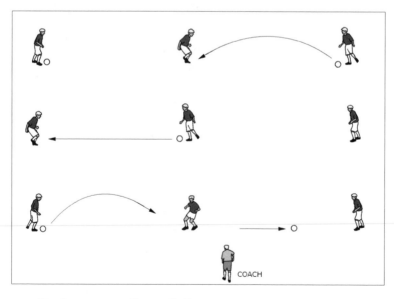

Equipment: Soccer Balls, cones.

Set-up: Three players in single file, approximately 10-15 yards apart. Two outside players and one middle player. The two outside players have a ball in their hands.

| *Activity:* | On the coach's command, the outside players alternate serving flighted balls to the middle player. The middle player receives the ball and plays it back to the server. |

Variations:

- The middle player plays it back with one touch or two touches.
- The middle player:
    - ✓ receives the ball with the instep, then plays it back to the server.
    - ✓ receives the ball with the inside/ outside of the foot (drag across body), then plays it back to the server.
    - ✓ prepares the ball close to the his body before playing it back to the server.
    - ✓ prepares the ball away from his body before playing it back to the server.
    - ✓ Heads or volleys the ball back to the server.
- Only one ball is used. On the coach's command, one of the outside players serves a flighted ball to the middle player, who must turn with the ball on the first touch and pass it to the opposite outside player.

Coaching Considerations: Proper receiving technique: good body balance, eyes on ball, body in-line with the path of the ball, movement to ball, appropriate touch on ball (cushion or propel).

144

◆ Short-Short-Long Passing (Pattern Passing)

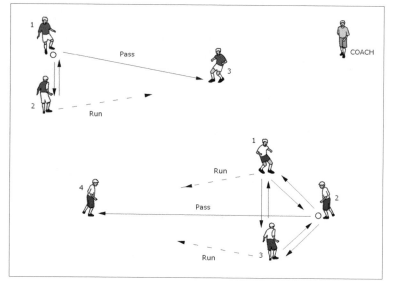

Equipment:	Soccer balls. Pinnies (2 or 3 different colors).
Set-up:	Open area. One ball per group of three.
Activity:	Players pass the ball within their group. Two of the players position themselves about 5-10 yards apart and pass the ball back and forth to each other (short passes), while the third player (long player) drifts/checks about 20-25 yards away. After 4-5 short passes, the long player calls for the ball. The ball is played into the long player. The player that played the ball to the long player stays home, while the other player joins the long player. They begin to (short) pass to each other until the new "long" player calls for the ball. The activity continues in this manner for 2-3 minutes to develop a smooth rhythm in the passing sequence. Players consistently keep themselves and the ball moving. (Develop a triangle shape)
Variations:	One ball per group of four. Similar to the activity described above, three players make short passes to each other, while one player drifts away. When the long ball is played, the passer stays home and the other two players join the "long" player. (Develop a "kite" type shape)

145

Intelligent movement, head up, preparing to receive the ball, surveying the area, looking for their target early, anticipation, passing accuracy and pace, keeping appropriate individual and group shape, playing in the direction that you are facing.

♦ Circle Passing (Two Balls)

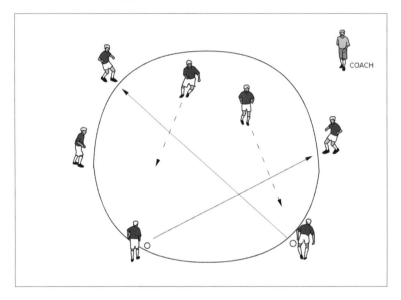

Equipment:	Soccer Balls.
Set-up:	All the players position themselves around the center circle or a circle with a radius of 10-15 yards. Two players have the soccer balls to begin the activity
Activity:	The players with the balls pass them to another player (it cannot be the players next to him), follows his pass and replaces the player he passed to. The player receiving the pass has two touches to control and pass the ball to someone else on the circle. He must also follow his pass and replace that player on the circle. The activity continues in this manner until the ball is played outside of the circle. Use Time as a challenge to the players; they must keep the ball moving, with the appropriate touches, inside the player circle for one minute!

Allow players one touch only.

Coaching Considerations: Intelligent movement, technical and tactical speed, head up, preparing to receive the ball, surveying the area, looking for their target early, anticipation, passing accuracy and pace, communication.

◆ Passing by the Numbers (Two Soccer Balls)

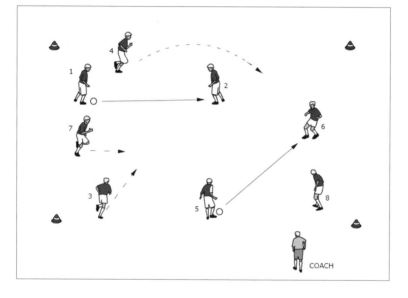

Equipment: Soccer balls. Pinnies (2 or 3 different colors).

Set-up: One ball per group of seven or eight players. The players in each group number themselves from one to seven (7) or from one to eight (8). Player number one and player number five each start with a ball at their feet.

Activity: On the coach's command, players pass the ball within their group by their consecutive numbers. At the same time that number one passes to two, and two passes to three, and three passes to four, etc., number five passes to six, then six passes to seven, etc. Two soccer balls are being played within each group. Players must be moving and the ball can never stop.

Coaching Considerations:

> Intelligent movement, head up, preparing to receive the ball, surveying the area, looking for their target early, anticipation, passing accuracy and pace, technical and tactical speed, communication.

♦ Inter-Passing in Groups (Shape)

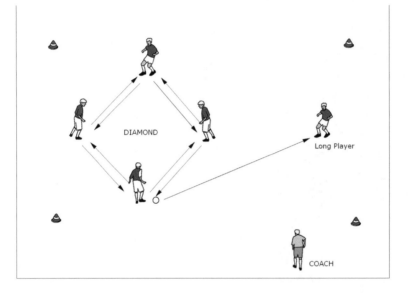

Equipment: Soccer balls. Pinnies (2 or 3 different colors).

Set-up: One ball per group of five.

Activity: Players pass the ball within their group. Four of the players position themselves about 10-15 yards apart, forming diamond shape (two central players and two outside players). They pass the ball back and forth to each other (short passes), while the fifth player (long player) positions himself/herself centrally about 25-30 yards away. After 4-5 short passes, the long player calls for the ball. The ball is played into the long player. The three players closest to the ball from the diamond move quickly to support the long player, forming the diamond shape at the other end of the grid. The deepest central player stays

148

home. The same passing sequence continues at the opposite end of the grid. The activity continues in this manner for 3-4 minutes to develop a smooth rhythm in the passing sequence. Players consistently keep themselves and the ball moving. (Developing a "kite" type shape)

Coaching Considerations:

Intelligent movement, head up, preparing to receive the ball, surveying the area, looking for their target early, anticipation, passing accuracy and pace, keeping appropriate individual and group shape, playing in the direction that you are facing.

♦ Middle Zone Shooting (Sequence Shooting)

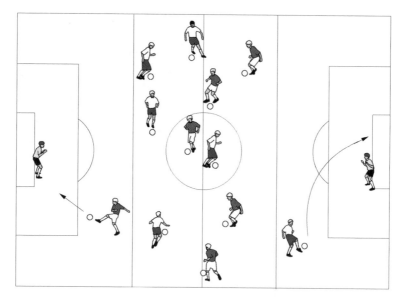

Equipment:	One ball per player, cones, goals.

| Set-up: | 70 yd x 40 yd rectangular field with goals at each end. Divide the field into three zones: 25 yd x 40 yd (end zone), 20 yd x 40 yd (middle zone), 25 yd x 40 yd (end zone). Separate players into two teams... yellow and red. Each player has a ball and has a consecutive number from one to six. Goalkeepers in each goal. The red team will shoot at one of the goals while the yellow team will shoot at the other goal. |

Activity: All players from both teams start out in the middle
zone dribbling through each other. On the coach's
command, red player #1 and yellow player #1 dribble
out of the middle zone toward their assigned goal and
shoot the ball. When they are safely out of the way
and returning to the middle zone, the #2's dribble
out of the middle zone and proceed to shoot on their
assigned goal. This sequence shooting continues
until many shot repetitions have been taken by all
players. The players must actively dribble while in
the middle zone.

Variation: The shooters can begin by taking medium paced
shots directly at the goalkeepers so that the keepers
can warm up properly and actively. Once the keepers
are warmed up, the shooters attempt to score goals.

Coaching Considerations:

Proper shooting technique, deceptive shooting
(toe, outside of the foot), long range and short
range shooting, placement of shots, speed of shot,
mechanical speed (speed of mechanics of shooting).

Dynamic Competitive Activities

◆ **Grid Combat with Bandits**

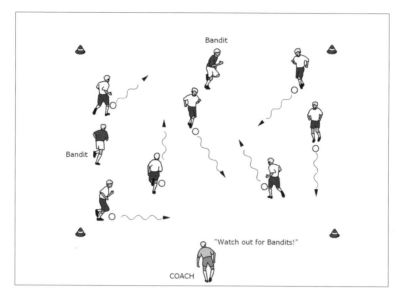

Equipment:	One ball per player and cones.
Set-up:	20 yd x 25 yd grid. All players in the grid. Every player has a ball at his feet (the dribblers), except two players (the bandits).
Activity:	On the coach's command, the dribblers move throughout the grid attempting to keep possession of their ball and avoid getting it stolen by one of the bandits. The bandits simply try to steal a ball from one of the dribblers. If a bandit steals a ball from one of the dribblers, he becomes a dribbler and the other player becomes a bandit. If a ball is kicked out of the grid, it is GONE, thus producing more bandits. Play multiple 1-2 minute(s) matches. When time is up, players with possession of a ball receive one point.
Variations:	Two players (passers) per ball. Each pair of players attempt to keep possession of their ball by dribbling and passing. The two bandits attempt to steal a ball. When a bandit steals a ball, he partners with the other bandit and become passers. The passers who lost possession of their ball become the bandits.

Dribbling under pressure, shielding, scheming, passing under pressure, communication with teammate, decisions to dribble or pass, defending, constructive tackling, winning possession of the ball.

♦ Timed Four versus Two Keep-Away (4v2)

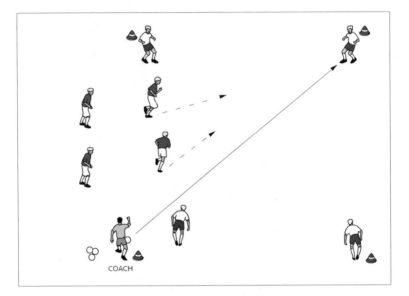

COACH

Equipment:	Soccer balls, cones, pinnies.
Set-up:	10 yd x 10 yd grid. Divide players into two or three color-coded teams; 4-5 players per team. If you have three teams, one team will rest while two of the teams will play. The 3rd team (blue) will be rotated in. Four players (attackers) from the red team position themselves in the grid. The yellow team (defenders) positions themselves outside the grid, on one side, in two single file lines. The coach is positioned near the yellow team (defenders) on one corner of the grid, equipped with six soccer balls. The coach appoints the assistant coach or a parent as the timekeeper.
Activity:	The coach proceeds to pass one ball into the grid. The timekeeper starts the clock. The first player in each of the yellow lines enters the grid. The four red players (attackers) attempt to keep the ball away

from the two yellow defenders. The defenders try to knock the ball out of the grid. If they do, they must exit the grid immediately and get back in their lines. *The clock continues to run.* Upon their exit, the coach passes the next ball into the grid. The next two yellow defenders enter the grid immediately and proceed to knock the ball out. This sequence continues until the coach has passed in all six balls. The same four red players (attackers) remain in the grid for all six balls. When the last ball is kicked out of the grid, time is stopped. The time for possession of the six balls is recorded for the red team. If there are three teams, the red team will rest, the yellow team will become the attackers and the blue team will become the defenders. Enough games should be played so that each team gets two attempts at defending and attacking. The winner is the team that has accumulated the most time on the clock while attacking.

Variations: Depending on the ability of your players, you can increase the number of players on each team and play 5 v 2 or you can increase the size of the grid (easier to possess) or decrease the size of the grid (harder to possess).

Coaching Considerations: Speed of play (technical and tactical speed), proper use of small space, destructive defending, fun!

◆ Timed Five versus Two Keep-Away (5v2)

COACH

Equipment:	Soccer balls, cones, pinnies.
Set-up:	Rectangular grid approximately 20 yards x 15 yards or a circle with similar area. Five players inside grid in red (attackers); two players inside the grid in yellow (defenders).
Activity:	On the coach's command the five red players attempt to keep the ball away from the two yellow players by passing or dribbling/shielding. The red team receives a point if they can successfully make five consecutive passes without the yellow players disrupting play or if they split the yellow players (pass the ball successfully to a teammate through the two yellow players).

If the play is disrupted, the red team gets a ball immediately and begins play again.

The yellow players receive one point if they knock the ball out of the area. They receive two points if they dribble or pass it out of the area under control.

Play multiple games, 2-3 min each, changing the defenders and attackers often. keep accumulated points for red and yellow for all the games.

Variations:	If you have enough players, you can have two games going. Seven red players and seven yellow players. This would allow five reds versus two yellows and five yellows versus two reds. After each game switch yellows and reds from one field to the other. Keep total accumulated points for each color.

Coaching Considerations:

Passing, receiving, dribbling, shielding, possession, technical and tactical speed, defending and transition.

♦ **Small-Sided Games with Neutral Players**

Equipment:	Soccer balls, pinnies, cones, flags and/or small goals.
Set-up:	Rectangular field, made with cones, approximately 40 yards long x 30 yards wide. Place goals made from cones, flags or ready-made goals at each end of the field. Separate players into two color-coded (red and yellow) groups (teams). Select one player who will wear a blue pinnie (neutral player). Send five players from each team to the field. The red players defend one goal at one end of the field and the yellow players defend the other goal. The blue player joins the field as a neutral player. The blue player only plays with the team in possession of the ball, giving

them a numerical advantage [i.e. 5 v 5+1 means: six attacking players versus five defending players].

Activity: On the coach's command, the red and yellow teams, along with the blue neutral players, play a 5 v 5+1 game. The players police themselves; in other words, they control the environment; they sort out rules, etc. The match lasts for 10-15 minutes.

Variation: Play 6 v 6+1 games. (Adjust fields appropriately)
Play 7 v 7+1 games. (Adjust fields appropriately)

Coaching Considerations:

Individual possession and possession in small groups (combination).
Individual and collective penetration; get in behind the opponents.
Pressure, cover and balance on defense; defending in two's, three's and four's.
Using the extra neutral players to your advantage.
Mentality; risky on the attack; restrained aggression on defense.

◆ Small-Sided Games with Free Flank Players

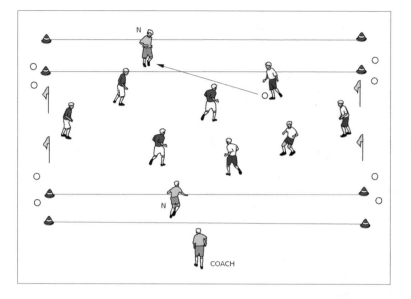

Equipment: Soccer balls, cones, flags, goals and pinnies.

Set-up: Rectangular field(s), 30 yards x 40 yards (adjust field size if necessary). Goals centered at each end of the field. Separate players into two color-coded (red and yellow) teams. Select one player from each team to be a flank player and outfit them in blue pinnies. Organize a 4 v 4 or 5 v 5 on the field of play (these numbers include the goalkeeper). Position the flank players, one on each side of the field, in lanes, outside the touch lines. The flank players can move freely in their lane and up and down the touch line, but cannot enter the field of play.

Activity: This is a typical 4 v 4 or 5 v 5 game, except that the flank players are totally free outside the field of play (no one from either team can pressure them). Either team can pass to a flank player. Once a flank player receives the ball from a team, he must play for that team and only has a maximum of 3 touches to return the ball into play to his team.

Variation: Play 5 v 5 or 6 v 6 with free flank players. (Adjust the field appropriately)
Position one red player and one yellow player in each flank to offer pressure to each other. Allow free switching of players from inside the field to the

flanks, but only one player from each team is allowed in the flank at any given time.

Coaching Considerations:

Crossing and heading opportunities. Finishing from crosses. Solving problems that only the game can provide.

♦ Zone 1 v 2 + 1 v 2 Competition

Equipment:	Soccer Balls, cones, pinnies, goals.
Set-up:	30 yd x 40 yd rectangular grid. Goals at each end with goalkeepers. Midfield line marked off with cones. Two teams, red and yellow. One red goalkeeper, one red defender and one yellow attacker positioned in ½ of the field (1 v 2); one yellow goalkeeper, one yellow defender and one red attacker in the other half of the field (1 v 2). Players must remain in their own half of the field.
Activity:	Game begins when one of the goalkeepers puts a ball in play by throwing it or kicking it off the ground. (no punting allowed by the goalkeeper). The goalkeeper and defender in one half attempt to combine with their attacker in the other half and score. Shots can be taken from anywhere on the field.

Variations:	Once a ball is played into the red attacker, the red defender can enter the other half and join the red attacker and once a ball is played into the yellow attacker, the yellow defender can enter the other half and join the yellow attacker.

Coaching Considerations:	Passing, receiving, combination play, shooting, defending, goalkeeper distribution, goalkeeper communication, goalkeeper foot skills.

♦ Zone 1 v 3 + 1 v 3 Competition

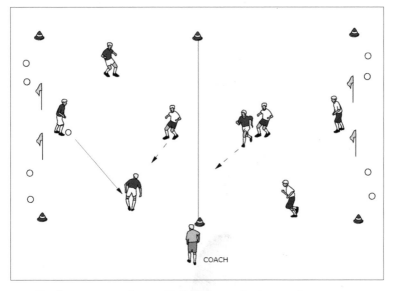

Equipment:	Soccer Balls, cones, pinnies, goals.
Set-up:	30 yd x 40 yd rectangular grid. Goals at each end with goalkeepers. Midfield line marked off with cones. Two teams, red and yellow. One red goalkeeper, two red defenders and one yellow attacker positioned in ½ of the field (1 v 3); one yellow goalkeeper, two yellow defenders and one red attacker in the other half of the field (1 v 3). Players must remain in their own half of the field. Multiple balls placed in each goal.
Activity:	Game begins when one of the goalkeepers puts a ball in play by throwing it or kicking it off the ground. (no

punting allowed by the goalkeeper). The goalkeeper and defenders in one half attempt to combine with their attacker in the other half and score. Shots can be taken from anywhere on the field.

Variations: Once a ball is played into the red attacker, a red defender can enter the other half and join the red attacker and once a ball is played into the yellow attacker, a yellow defender can enter the other half and join the yellow attacker.

Coaching Considerations: Passing, receiving, combination play, shooting, defending, goalkeeper distribution, goalkeeper communication, goalkeeper foot skills, group attacking and defending shape.

◆ Zone 2 v 3 + 2 v 3 Competition

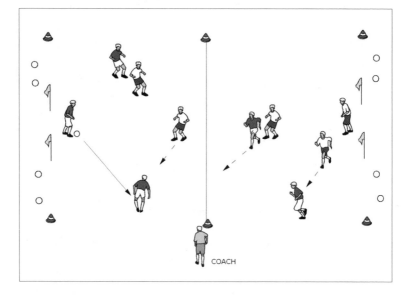

Equipment: Soccer Balls, cones, pinnies, goals.

Set-up: 40 yd x 45 yd rectangular grid. Goals at each end with goalkeepers. Midfield line marked off with cones. Two teams, red and yellow. One red goalkeeper, two red defenders and two yellow attackers positioned in ½ of the field (2 v 3); one yellow goalkeeper, two yellow defenders and two red attackers in the other half of the field (2 v 3). Players must remain in their own half of the field. Multiple balls placed in each goal.

Activity: Game begins when one of the goalkeepers puts a ball in play by throwing it or kicking it off the ground. (no punting allowed by the goalkeeper). The goalkeeper and defenders in one half attempt to combine with their attackers in the other half and score. Shots can be taken from anywhere on the field.

Variations: Once a ball is played into a red attacker, a red defender can enter the other half and join the red attackers and once a ball is played into a yellow attacker, a yellow defender can enter the other half and join the yellow attackers.

Coaching Considerations: Passing, receiving, combination play, shooting, defending, goalkeeper distribution, goalkeeper communication, goalkeeper foot skills, group attacking and defending shape.

161

◆ Zone 2v4 + 2v4 Competition

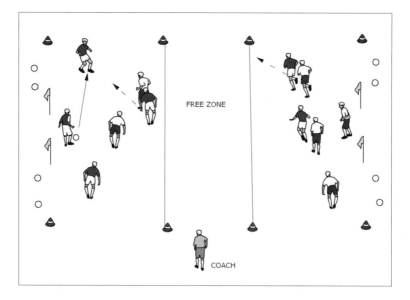

Equipment: Soccer balls, cones, pinnies, goals.

Set-up: 70 yd x 40 yd rectangular field with goals at each end. Divide the field into three zones: 25 yd x 40 yd (end zone), 20 yd x 40 yd (middle zone or free zone), 25 yd x 40 yd (end zone). Goalkeepers in each goal. Two teams, red and yellow. One red goalkeeper, three red defenders and two yellow attackers positioned in one end zone (2 v 4); one yellow goalkeeper, three yellow defenders and two red attackers in the other end zone (2 v 4). Attackers must remain in their end zone. Multiple balls placed in each goal.

Activity: Game begins when one of the goalkeepers puts a ball into play by throwing it or kicking it off the ground. (no punting allowed by the goalkeeper). The goalkeeper and defenders in one end-zone attempt to combine with their attackers in the other end-zone and score. They can do this by directly making a pass through the free zone to their attackers; or one of the defenders can dribble into the free zone and take a long range shot or pass it to their attackers from there. A defender can only enter the free zone if he has possession of the ball. If this is the case, no one else can enter the free zone. Once in the free zone the defender has only 3 touches to pass or shoot the ball.

When the defender does so, he must return to his end zone. Shots can be taken from anywhere on the field.

Variations: Once a ball is played into a red attacker, a red defender can enter the other end zone and join the red attackers and once a ball is played into a yellow attacker, a yellow defender can enter the other end zone and join the yellow attackers.

Coaching Considerations: Passing, receiving, combination play, shooting, defending, goalkeeper distribution, goalkeeper communication, goalkeeper foot skills, playing out of the back by the defenders, group attacking and defending shape.

◆ Shooting with Uneven Numbers

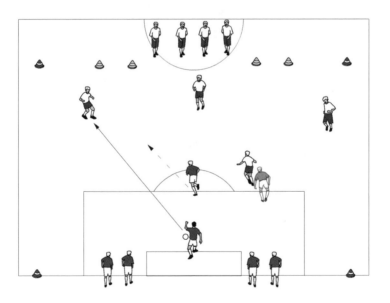

Equipment: Soccer balls, cones, flags, goals and pinnies.

Set-up: Rectangular grid 40 yards wide x 35 yards long (wider than long). A goal centered at one end of the field and two counter attack goals (made from flags or cones) positioned just inside the corners at the opposite end of the field. Separate your players into two groups. Put one third of the players in yellow pinnies (defenders and goalkeepers); put the remaining two thirds of your players in red pinnies (attackers). Select four attackers and three defenders to compete. The four attackers space themselves out at the end of the field opposite from the goal. The defenders take up positions at the other end of the field. One of the defenders acts as a goalkeeper, but must play with his feet whenever possible (4 v 3). The coach can set up two of these field spaces, if necessary, to get more player involvement.

Activity: The goalkeeper starts the competition by kicking the ball (punt or from the ground) in the direction of the attackers. The 4 v 3 begins. The four attackers attempt to score on the goal (1 point awarded). The three defenders attempt to win possession of the ball and kick it through one of the counter-attack goals (2 points awarded). Competitions should last a maximum of 2 minutes. Rotate players in appropriately.

Variations: Play with different numbers (5 v 4, 6 v 5, etc.) Adjust the field space to suit the number of players..

Coaching Considerations:

Technical speed (dribbling, receiving, passing, heading, shooting, tackling) under pressure, tactical speed under pressure (when, where, how, why?), playing with numbers up, playing with numbers down.

◆ Four Corner Shooting

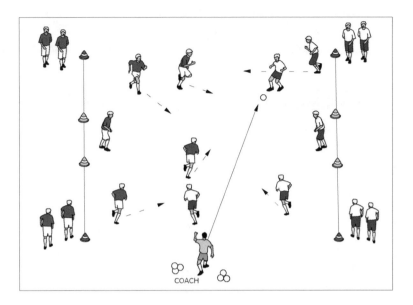

Equipment: Enough soccer balls for all players, pinnies, goals, cones and flags if available.

Set-up: 30 yard x 25 yard rectangular grid (field). Goals at each end of the field. Coach positioned outside the field at the mid-line with all of the balls. Two teams of players, in different colored pinnies; half of each team lined up in single file behind a specified corner cone (4 lines); one team at one end and one team at the other end. Goals are designated for each team and goalkeepers are positioned in each goal.

Activity: When the coach serves a ball into the field of play, the first 2 players in each of the four lines enters the field and a 5 v 5 competition begins (4 field players and a goalkeeper for each team). Play continues until a goal is scored or the ball goes out of bounds. When this happens, the players must get off the field quickly and get back in their line. When they are off the field, the coach sends another ball into the field, and the competition continues with the next players in each line. Play continues in this manner until all of the balls are used up. At this point, the coach says that he is out of soccer balls and asks all the players to go get a ball and dribble it back to him. Once the balls are collected, a new round of play begins.

Coaching Considerations:

Technique under the pressure of a game, decision making in the competitive game environment, triangular and rectangular shapes, passing and receiving, shooting, FUN!

◆ The Game 8v8

COACH

Equipment:	Enough balls for all players, cones and flags if available.
Set-up:	50 yard x 75 yard rectangular grid (field). Goals at each end made out of cones or flags, approximately 5-6 steps wide. Balls are placed outside and behind the goals. 8v8 on the field.
Activity:	Start play with a kick-off from the center of the field. Use US Youth Soccer modified rules.

166

Coaching Considerations

Technique

Dribbling

Low, balanced body position.
Agile lateral (left-to-right) movement for dribbling in tight spaces, change of direction and faking out opponents.
Proper use of insides and outsides of the feet and the toe to propel ball an appropriate distance.
Proper use of soles of the feet to pull, push and roll the ball.
Eyes up enough to survey the situation and to have good peripheral vision.
Keep the ball close when under pressure (lots of touches).
Propel the ball away from feet when dribbling into space away from pressure.

Receiving

Coaching Points (common to all surfaces)

Keep body relaxed.
Eyes on the ball while it is traveling and as you receive it.
Position body in-line with the in-coming ball.
Present a surface to receive the ball with.
Cushion the ball if it arrives with velocity.
Propel the ball away if it arrives slowly or if under pressure or in open field.

Coaching Points (unique to specific receiving surfaces)

Sole of the Foot

Ground Ball
Comfortable body position.
One foot on the ground.
Present the sole of the foot at about a 45 degree angle to the ground as the ball arrives.
Wedge the in-coming ball between the sole and the ground.

Flighted Ball (Angled/vertical arrival)
Comfortable body position.
One foot on the ground.
Allow the ball to hit the ground.
Just as the ball hits the ground, present the sole of the foot over the ball (wedge the ball between the sole of the foot and the ground).

167

Inside of the Foot

Ground Ball
Comfortable body position.
One foot on the ground.
Present the inside of the foot to the in-coming ball.
Pull the receiving foot back or propel it forward depending on the velocity of the ball.

Flighted Ball (Angled/vertical arrival)
Comfortable body position.
One foot on the ground.
Allow the ball to hit the ground.
Just as the ball hits the ground, present the inside of foot over the ball and drag the ball away from pressure.

Line-Drive Ball (Horizontal arrival)
Comfortable body position.
One foot on the ground.
Present the inside of the foot to the in-coming ball.
Pull the receiving foot back or propel it forward depending on the velocity of the ball.

Outside of the Foot

Ground Ball
Comfortable body position.
One foot on the ground.
Present the outside of the foot to the in-coming ball.
Pull the receiving foot back or propel it forward depending on the velocity of the ball.

Flighted Ball (Angled/vertical arrival)
Comfortable body position.
One foot on the ground.
Allow the ball to hit the ground.
Just as the ball hits the ground, present the outside of foot over the ball and drag the ball away from pressure.

Laces (In-step)

Flighted Ball (Angled/vertical arrival)
Comfortable body position.
One foot on the ground.
Present the laces to the in-coming ball.
Lower foot (give with the foot) as ball is received.

168

Thigh

Flighted Ball (Angled/vertical arrival)
Comfortable body position.
Straight back.
One foot on the ground.
Present the mid/upper thigh (horizontal to the ground) to the in-coming ball.
Lower thigh (give with the thigh) as ball is received.

Line-Drive Ball (Horizontal arrival)
Comfortable body position.
One foot on the ground.
Present the mid/upper thigh (perpendicular to the ground) to the in-coming ball.
Pull the receiving thigh or propel it forward depending on the velocity of the ball.

Chest

Flighted Ball (Angled/vertical arrival)
Comfortable body position.
Arch back (limbo dance position).
Arms out.
Both feet on the ground or both feet off ground (if jumping).
Present the chest (45-60 degree angle to the ground) to the in-coming ball.
Bend the knees to absorb the ball (cushion) as it is received.

Line-Drive Ball (Horizontal arrival)
Comfortable body position.
Straight back.
Arms out.
Both feet on the ground or both feet off ground (if jumping).
Present the chest (perpendicular to the ground) to the in-coming ball.
Jump back to absorb the ball (cushion) as it is received.

Kicking (Passing and Shooting)

Coaching Points (common to kicking low/ground balls)

Low/Ground Balls

Non-kicking foot placed comfortably next to the ball.
Non-kicking foot pointed in the direction of the target.
Body slightly over the ball.
Knee of kicking leg slightly over the ball.
Eyes on ball.
Land on the kicking foot.

Coaching Points (unique to specific kicking surfaces)

Inside of foot

Lock ankle with toe pointed up on kicking foot.
Straight kick… Strike through the center (equator) or slightly above the center of the ball with the ankle surface of the foot.
Bent kick… Strike/Slice the outside center (or slightly below center) of the ball with the inside of the foot.

Instep (laces)

Lock ankle with toe pointed down on kicking foot.
Strike ball with instep surface of the foot.

Outside of the foot (for deceptive passes and shots)

Non-kicking foot placed slightly farther away from the ball than normal.
Lock ankle with toe pointed down and turned in.

Straight kick… Strike (punch) the inside center (or slightly above center) of the ball with the outside of the foot.
Bent kick… Strike/Slice the inside center (or slightly below center) of the ball with the outside of the foot.

Coaching Points (common to kicking flighted/air balls)

Flighted/Air Balls

Approach ball from slight angle.
Non-kicking foot placed comfortably next to and slightly behind the ball.
Non-kicking foot pointed in the direction of the target.
Body upright and slightly leaning back..
Eyes on ball.
Strike with laces or upper inside surface of the foot.
Strike through the bottom/center of the ball.
Land on the kicking foot.

Coaching Points (unique to specific types of kicks)

Chip

Lock ankle with toe pointed up on kicking foot.
Sharply cut the grass below the ball with the kicking foot (like a 9-iron or wedge shot in golf).
The ball should travel with backspin.

Long/Driven ball

Big power step (step right before the kick is taken).
Lock ankle with toe pointed down on kicking foot.
Strike ball with instep surface of the foot.

Outside of the foot (for deceptive passes and shots)

Non-kicking foot placed slightly farther away from the ball than normal.
Lock ankle with toe pointed down and turned in.

Bent kick...Strike/Slice the ball below the inside center with the outside of the foot.

Heading

Square the body to the ball (body in line with the in-coming ball).
Eyes on ball.
Time the jump if one is necessary.
Tighten the neck muscles.
Arch the back.
Arms out and forward for balance.
Thrust upper body forward.
Contact the ball with the top of the forehead.
The head strikes the ball! (like the hammer hits the nail)

To drive the ball down... strike the upper half of the ball.
To drive the ball up... strike the lower half of the ball.

Tackling

Block tackle

Maintain a comfortable playing distance from the opponent.
Do not telegraph your intent.
Shepard the opponent to one side or the other.
Do not commit yourself too early (do not dive in)...time your execution.
Throw stabbing fakes at the opponent to force mistakes.
Keep your eyes on the ball.
Keep a low center of gravity.
One foot slightly angled in front of the other with bent knees; back foot is the tackling foot; front foot is the plant/balancing foot.
When tackling, place the front foot to the side of the ball (as if to make an inside of the foot pass).
Use the inside of the back foot to drag through the ball keeping the ankle locked, toe up and knee bent.
Lower same side shoulder (as tackling foot) thrusting it forward to provide the necessary forward momentum and velocity to handle the impact of the opponent's force.
Drag the ball through and into the space behind the opponent and start the attack!

Toe Poke

Same as Block Tackling with the following exception:

Use the toe of the front foot to poke the ball away!

172

Tactics

*There are three **moments** in the game of soccer:*

> When your team has possession of the ball (attacking)…
> When your team does not have possession of the ball (defending)…
> When your team is changing from one to the other (transition)…

Tactics *refers to the decisions that players make in the heat of the competition in each of these **moments**.*

The progression in teaching tactics to our players must be gradual and proceed from simple to complex. This is best achieved by providing playing environments that train:

> Individual tactics
> Small group tactics
> Team tactics

Coaches must understand the Principles of the game to effectively teach tactics:

> Attacking Principles
> Defending Principles
> Transition

Important player terminology:

> 1st Attacker…player in possession of the ball; responsible for penetration.
> 2nd Attackers…players near the 1st Attacker; responsible for support .
> 3rd Attackers…players away from the 1st attacker; responsible for mobility and providing width and length.

Attacking Principles

Penetration

Advancing the ball forward into the space behind the defending team.
Responsibility of the **1ˢᵗ attacker** (player in possession of the ball).

This is accomplished by dribbling, passing or shooting the ball:

> *Recognize that there is space behind the defending team to exploit.*
> *Dribble by an opponent(s) using deceptive moves, change of speed and direction.*
> *Passing to a teammate in a forward position or running into the space behind the defending team.*
> *Shooting at the opponents goal.*

Support

Providing help to the 1ˢᵗ attacker in the area around the ball.
Responsibility of the **2ⁿᵈ attackers** (attacking players in close proximity to the ball).

This is accomplished by:

> *Recognizing that the 1ˢᵗ attacker needs help.*
> *Communicating with the 1ˢᵗ attacker...*
> *alerting the 1ˢᵗ attacker that you are available and where you are or will be.*
> *Timing your runs...moving to a supporting position at the right time...not to early-not too late.*
> *Being at the right angle and distance to support the 1ˢᵗ attacker...behind, square or in advance of the ball.*
> *Providing good body shape...positioning your body so that you can keep the attack moving in a positive direction (forward toward the opposing goal).*

Mobility

Team movement provided by the attacking players close to the ball (2nd attackers) and away from the ball (**3rd attackers**).

This is accomplished with:

Short, explosive runs (angled and lateral).
Checking runs…away from the ball, then quickly back to the ball.
Deceptive, long runs out of the back.
Overlapping runs.

Shape

The attacking look or make-up of the team at any point in time with regards to positioning. Determined by where the ball is and where & how pressure is being applied by the defending team.

The attacking team must provide width, length and connection:

Width…*players moving into positions that widen the field. Players moving into positions that allow them to use as much of the field as possible. Opening the field up laterally (from East to West).*

Length…*players moving into positions that lengthen the field. Players moving into positions that allow them to use as much of the field as possible. Opening the field up vertically (from North to South).*

Connection…*players in positions to link or connect players from East to West and North to South. Usually midfield players.*

Improvisation

The innate ability by a player or players to solve a soccer problem with flair and creativity.

Defending Principles

Pressure

> The action of the **1st defender** (defender closest to the ball).
>
> The responsibilities include:
>
> > **To intercept the ball** and win possession for his team.
> > **To tackle the opponent** and win possession for his team.
> > **To delay the forward progress** by the 1st attacker and thus for the attacking team.

Cover

> Providing help to the 1st defender in the area around the ball.
> Responsibility of the **2nd defenders** (defending players in close proximity to the ball).
>
> This is accomplished by:
>
> > Taking a position at an appropriate angle and distance behind the 1st defender to:
> >
> > > Prevent penetration by the 1st attacker with the pass (prevent splitting the 1st and 2nd defenders).
> > > Become the pressuring defender if the 1st defender gets beat.
> > > Match up with (track and/or mark) the 2nd attacker.
>
> The tighter the pressure being applied by the 1st defender...the tighter (closer) the cover by the 2nd defender.
>
> The looser the pressure being applied by the 1st defender...the looser (farther away) the cover by the 2nd defender.

Balance

> Providing defensive help and safety at a distance away from the ball.

This is the responsibility of the **3rd defenders** (players away from the ball). They must:

> *Track (keep an eye on) attackers away from the ball.*
>
> *Position themselves so that they can squeeze space centrally, making the field smaller for the attacking team.*
>
> *Position themselves so that they can become the 1st or 2nd defender immediately if a pass is made by the attacking team.*

Shape

The defensive look or make-up of the team at any point in time with regards to positioning. Determined by where the ball is and how the attacking shape is organized.

The defending team must be compact (concentrated) between the ball and their goal. This will help to prevent penetration by the attacking team.

Transition

This is the moment in the game when players must change their mentality (their roles) from attacking to defending or defending to attacking. Teams that can accomplish this with speed and organization are successful.

Resources

Goodman, Tom, M.Ed., Soccer Skills Technique…Practice Sessions for Coaches, World Class Soccer, Inc., 1990

Kidman, Lynn, developing decision makers…An Empowerment Approach to Coaching, pp.118-130. P.O. Box 31 259, Christchurch, New Zealand: Innovative Print Communications Ltd., 2001

Quinn, Dr. Ronald W., THE PEAK PERFORMANCE Soccer Games for Player Development, QSM Consultants, 1990

United States Soccer Federation, National C License Curriculum Manual, 2003

United States Soccer Federation, National B License Curriculum Manual, 2003

United States Soccer Federation, National A License Curriculum Manual, 2003

United States Soccer federation, National Youth License Manual, 2004

Willis, Mariaemma, M.S. & Hodson, Victoria Kindle, M.A., Discover Your Child's Learning Style, Prima Publishing, 1999

Activities Index

Z